EXPLORING CAREERS IN SPECIAL EDUCATION

EXPLORING CAREERS
IN SPECIAL EDUCATION

By

Marilyn Jones

RICHARDS ROSEN PRESS, INC.
New York, N.Y. 10010

Published in 1981 by Richards Rosen Press, Inc.
29 East 21st Street, New York, N.Y. 10010

First Edition

Library of Congress Cataloging in Publication Data

Jones, Marilyn.
    Exploring careers in special education.

    Bibliography: p.
    1. Teachers of handicapped children—Vocational
guidance. 2. Learning disabilities. 3. Problem
children—Education. I. Title.
LC4704.J66   371.9   80–29101
ISBN 0–8239–0539–X

Manufactured in the United States of America

Dedicated to the 43rd St. Neighborhood Kids, whom I do not teach, but who are so important to my life:
Chris, Mark, Charles, Ronnie, Marcie, Ignatius, Tasha, Cheryl and Eric and Gloria and Keith and Angie

About the Author

Marilyn Jones has been a teacher for twenty-six years in five States: New York, New Jersey, Ohio, West Virginia, and Kentucky. She has taught every grade from one to eight in the regular program and in grades six to twelve in special education. For several years she taught in an alternative school for truants and behavior-problem children. For thirteen years as a member of a religious order, she taught in Catholic schools, and during two of those years she was housemother for twelve teen-

age boys in an orphanage. She has also been a counselor at a school for handicapped children and has conducted workshops for teachers and parents of the handicapped.

Miss Jones lives in an old house in Louisville, Kentucky, with an assortment of stray cats and dogs that have happened along, and with the companionship of some wonderful neighborhood children whom she counts among her best friends. At times she has had foster children in her home, all of whom had serious emotional problems and one of whom was educationally deprived.

Miss Jones has a touching—albeit sad—footnote to the story in Chapter IX about the "School That Hummed." The parents of the school's pupils sued the board of education, challenging its right to close the school. On the night before the judge was to make the final decision on the suit, a group of parents and teachers met and had read aloud to them an account of the school's activities and remarkable results. Each time the narrator came to a mention of the "hum" in the school, everyone in the audience hummed. There were tears and a lot of choked voices. Sadly, the judge ruled in favor of the board, but the "School That Hummed" is still not forgotten.

Contents

EXPLORING CAREERS IN SPECIAL EDUCATION

Chapter I

Learning Disabled Kids Express Their Feelings About Learning Disabilities

There are certainly plenty of opportunities for jobs if you want to become a teacher of the Learning Disabled or the Behavior Disordered child. More and more teachers are needed for these fields every year. We seem to be "finding" more and more children who have learning problems or who are disruptive in regular classes. The need for special ed. classes for LD-BD students is growing, growing, growing.

"Marvelous!" you say. "A field with endless job opportunities," you say.

Wait! Before you rush right out and commit your life to a career in the special ed. classrooms of the world, let me share with you the viewpoints of some "insiders" from this system. The following is a transcript of a conversation I had with some of my LD students. We began by discussing a portion of the book *Put Your Mother on the Ceiling* by Richard DeMille. There is an exercise in imaginative thinking in the book in which we "breathed fire" on some objects of our choosing and totally destroyed those things. Listen:

Question: Which exercise did you like best in *Put Your Mother on the Ceiling?*
BEN: Destroying.
ADAM: Fire.
Question: What did you want to destroy?
KIT: School.
ADAM: If you really want to breathe in fire—really come true—you can blow up the whole school.
Question: Why do you hate school so much?

3

BEN: Because I fail.

LYDIA: It ain't no fun.

ALICE: You get in trouble all the time.

Question: If you were the smartest kid in your class, would you hate school?

ADAM: I am the smartest kid in my class.

KIT: I made 100 points in reading.

LYDIA: One time I read twice and made 200 points.

Question: Do you like to read?

LYDIA: Yup.

ALICE: Yeah.

ADAM: I like to read about wolf stories.

CHUCK: Some words I don't know and people help me. I can read lots of words, but some I just pass up. Sometime I be reading and, you know, there's a hard word I can't get—I just keep on reading on the other words beside them and then it'll come to me what the word is.

BEN: Just like that one day—I read that story about the brain. I figured out about six words that I didn't know.

Question: Why do you hate to come to this class for reading?

CHUCK: Because sometimes I be mad when I come in here 'cause people be talking about me.

ADAM: Yeah, LD dummies. *Little Dummies.*

BEN: Well, if they say that to me, I really don't care if they do. It don't hurt me—

Question: Sticks and stones will break my bones, but words will never hurt me. Is that true?

ALICE: Uhh-no. (shakes head no)

CHUCK: Half of it is true, and half of it is not.

BEN: When they in their class and they call you little dummy, they ain't doing any better'n what you're doing.

ADAM: I feel like beheading those kids.

ALICE: De-brain them.

Question: Put them on the ceiling? Do you want to put them on the ceiling?

KIT: Then we could have our classes down here and be the smartest ones.

LYDIA: In regular classrooms, though, you can't come out and tell everybody what your problem is and in these classes you can.

CHUCK: You can be honest about yourself in here.

ALICE: They take out more time and discuss your problem with you.

BEN: You can feel free to say what you think.

ADAM: I feel like the teacher doesn't lie to me in LD.

BEN: The teachers in here come out with straight answers and stuff. I mean they don't hesitate or nothing like that.

Question: In the regular program they lie to you?

ADAM: I've had a couple teachers lie to me. Like they won't come out with the straight truth, you know. They tell you you're doing a good job—and you're not—and you find you're in LD.

LYDIA: They got people in our class that don't do no work. They ain't in LD. They should be.

BEN: They always playing.

KIT: There's some people that should be in LD, and I should be in their class.

CHUCK: There's too many of them like that in that class. They don't do none of their work, like we be doing most of what they be doing in their room.

Question: Does it make you mad then that you're here and they get to stay in the regular program?

ADAM: Yeah.

CHUCK: At least you be learning more in here.

KIT: They're all show-offs.

ADAM: I've been in LD all my life.

BEN: This is my first year ever, ever in LD.

CHUCK: I've been in LD since second grade.

BEN: They put me in here for back-talking teachers.

ALICE: They put me in here because of my behavior.

LYDIA: They took me out of my math class and put me in here because I came late and didn't do all my work.

CHUCK: I'm in LD because I cut classes all the time.

LYDIA: We do the same thing in here that the other people do.

KIT: In reading I'm doing everything they're doing.

BEN: The reason I'm in LD is, you know, the teacher says if you have a problem raise your hand, so I raise my hand and they never come—so I just walk away. I just throw my paper away.

KIT: The reason why they said they put me in LD is 'cause I used to be real quiet. I'd get my work done, but I didn't talk a lot and stuff. I used to be scared, so they put me in LD.

ALICE: They took me out for a little while, but I got put back in last year.

BEN: We seen movies practically every day in my class last year in LD. Practically every day.

CHUCK: In the other school I went to, every Thursday and Friday in LD they'd show movies.

BEN: They show cartoons and then take field trips.

ADAM: If we don't do any work, it makes me feel like we're dummies.

KIT: We did a little work.

BEN: To me LD is for the slower learners who can't get up with the higher grades.

ALICE: You get behind, so when you go to LD they try to get you up to your grade. If you can get good grades long enough, they probably try you out in the regular classes again.

BEN: Then if you start dropping back down, you come in here again.

ALICE: I used to read a book a day in my other school. I was doing real good and was ready to come out of LD, then the regular teacher started messing with me, and me and him got into it, so I'm in LD again.

CHUCK: The worst part of being in LD is when you get your report card and it's got LD on it.

ADAM: Yeah, I hate that.

BEN: My teacher gets real mad when they announce the LD kids have to stay in her class all period for something. She gets all mad.

Question: Do you feel you can read well enough to do every bit of work in the regular program?

ADAM: Yeah.

BEN: I do.

KIT: I know I can.

Question: Then words are not your enemy anymore?

BEN: No.

Question: Do you like words? Do you feel you can handle any word that's thrown at you?

KIT: Yeah.

BEN: If I try.

KIT: My teacher says I can read and stuff.

CHUCK: I got three reading classes.

Question: Do you think you can remember your reading clues, like the ce, ci, cy sounds?

CHUCK: That's what helped me in my regular class. We been reading books. That's what helped me—those charts. (phonics charts)

LYDIA: He does read good in her room.

Question: Why are you in here?

ALICE: My behavior.

BEN: She didn't tell us we were in a third-grade book till last week.

KIT: When we get out of LD, I hope we'll be on our right reading level.

Question: Why do you think words have been such a problem to you.

LYDIA: I didn't know where to break up the long words.

BEN: We didn't know how to put the sounds in the right order.

CHUCK: I never heard some of those words.

ADAM: Teachers should read to us—

BEN: How do you get a learning disability?

CHUCK: I don't know. It started when you was born, I guess.

ADAM: No, it didn't. I got it when I was in first grade. I didn't want to learn.

ALICE: LD is—that you can learn, but you learn slow.

KIT: I'm not slower than other kids in my room.

LYDIA: Those other kids probably just didn't want to get in here

KIT: I didn't want to get in here.

CHUCK: They just told me to come in here, and I came in here.

BEN: We play too much to keep up.

ADAM: This guy in our room can't read at all, and he's not in LD. Everybody reads better'n him and he's not in LD.

BEN: When I ask the teacher for help, they don't help you or nothin'.

KIT: Like—if you like the class you're in, you still have to leave and come up here and do the same stuff till you get out on your level.

BEN: It would be nice if you could come up here just when you want to or feel you need to.

ADAM: Some of us have been in here so long, we don't care if we get out.

ALICE: Sometimes LD is harder than the regular program.

LYDIA: If you hurry up and get out you might forget everything.

ADAM: I want to get out, but I don't know if I could make it, I've been in LD so long. I've been in LD eight years.

BEN: I wish I could get out of LD. Right now. Right today.

CHUCK: I'd leave this very minute if I could.

If you still think you'd like a job in special education as an LD or a BD teacher, we'll investigate further some of the problem areas that Ben and Alice and Chuck and the others touched on in the chapters that follow. Why do they feel the way they do, and can you help them to resolve their problems?

The students in this transcript are middle school students, sixth, seventh and eighth graders. Their names have been changed for their own protection, but they are very, very real and very, very typical.

Chapter **II**

Defining the Problem of Learning-Behavior Disorders

BEN: *How do you get a learning disability?*

It could be a disease for all they know, these kids to whom an LD or a BD classification has been given. In fact, BD kids are sometimes referred to as "cured" when their "treatment" time in special ed. has been successful and they can go back to regular classes.

Are these kids "different" from other kids, from their friends in the mainstream? What has happened to them along the way that they had to be singled out for special treatment?

In most ordinary schools of most ordinary school districts, these kids are not that much different from their counterparts in the mainstream. And it's probably fair to say that just about all kids have to deal with some kinds of problems in growing up—in growing up in this particular world at this unique time, anyway. For some, those problems are particularly related to school; depending upon how successfully they can seem to manage, they will be "regular" kids or be singled out for help in special programs.

Part of the confusion that Ben and Adam and their friends expressed in their conversation stems from the fact that they themselves know that they are not very much different from their friends in regular classes. In fact, it is obvious to them that a significant number of their mainstream classmates are in worse shape than they themselves. This, then, creates a new problem for them, adds to their unhappiness, increases their stress. Sometimes they feel they have just plain been treated unfairly. How could this have happened to them? How did they get here? Will they ever get out?

9

1. Super Kid

And really, when you get to know them, these kids are terrific kids. They are funny, and loving, and lovable, and playful, and mischievous, and smart. They like to play tricks on others, like to have their own way, like to giggle and tell jokes, like to sneak candy into class, and like to cheat on their homework. They hate to write stories, hate to do reading problems in arithmetic, hate to sit still for very long, hate to be bored. Some of them hate to read out loud. They all hate to spell.

But that could be you, couldn't it? Probably you have a friend or a brother or a sister who is a lot like that description. You know this is the normal way for a normal kid to be. You're right.

It's just that, for these kids, one or two or several of these characteristics became a problem for somebody somewhere along the line. For somebody. Somebody else, maybe. Or maybe for themselves.

The kid who is always out of the seat in class, throws mashed potatoes and peas at other kids in the lunchroom, talks all day long, and is reading way, way below grade level has a problem. And so does the child's teacher. And the teacher knows that one way to solve this problem is to have an evaluation done for the child, an evaluation that may result in special ed. placement. That is one way of solving the problem. That is the solution that was decided upon for Ben and Adam and Kit and the others.

They were, as the textbooks say, hyperactive, or had short attention spans, or were easily distracted. Someone who is hyperactive, has a short attention span, is easily distracted, and who is having a bad time of it in reading and math and spelling and writing is a pretty good candidate for an LD or a BD class, depending on which is more serious, the learning problem or the behavior problem.

Actually, our friends knew enough about themselves, and had thought it through enough, to have figured out pretty much what had happened to them. Alice knew, for instance, that she was in the LD room primarily because her behavior had affected her learning achievement. Ben said that they put him in there for back-talking teachers. Lydia knew that she didn't make up her math work and got behind. Kit was aware of her problem; she had been so quiet and afraid that she didn't respond adequately in class.

The thing that really hurts them is that they see everyone else's behavior as being significantly no different from their own. And, in all likelihood, that is probably so. The possibility exists that their special ed. referrals were the results of "straws that broke the camel's back." They acted out or performed poorly in an educational capacity "at the wrong place, at the wrong time." Someone else couldn't cope with them any longer.

> The child was killed at nine o'clock
> on the morning they read the evaluation.
> His teachers, and all, they'd taken stock
> and referred him to special education.
> "You won't mind this so much, you know,"
> they assured him. "And you can get back

in the mainstream as soon as you show
you've learned the skills you sorely lack."

But the current always flowed against him.
He couldn't swim when tides were low.
When he tried to catch the mainstream,
They'd drag him back to shore in tow.
He fell further back. They plunged way ahead.
They would never stop and wait for him.
He was captured here in special ed.,
sinking, drowning, apart from the mainstream.

The referrals go in. The testing gets done. Usually school systems have testing teams to do the evaluations. A psychometrist will do the psychological testing. Specially trained teachers can do the educational testing, the testing that shows what grade level a child is on in certain areas, say, reading and math. Then someone from the team will observe the child in a few classes, or in the halls, or in the lunchroom to see what the behavior and performance are like.

But what happens if it just turns out to be a bad day for a kid on testing day? What if the check didn't come in on time yesterday and Chuck's mother fussed at him all last night and this morning? What if he didn't have anything to eat at home, overslept this morning, and got to school so late that he missed breakfast here?

Or what if Lydia and her best friend had a fight before school this morning and her friend is telling everyone that Lydia broke into her locker and stole some money?

What if the bus driver reported Adam to the principal this morning for his behavior on the bus?

Or maybe this day is no different from any other. Maybe on this testing day, as on every other day, a child has been called "dirt" by friends, abused by parents, hollered at, ignored, bullied, mocked, teased, misunderstood. Maybe, on this testing day, as on every other day, the child reads the teacher's dislike from facial expressions, angry gestures, abruptness. The child knows the cold, grudging, nasty attitude the teacher has for him long before testing day. The child knows the teacher can't stand to touch her, bend over her desk and help her, or even hand her papers back nicely, long before testing day. Testing day may be just one more miserable, confused, unhappy day in the midst of a year full, or a life full, of miserable, confused, unhappy days for a child.

How then can a child's intelligence be measured on such a day, or on any day, by a stranger who brings forms to fill out about him, and who has booklets for him to fill, or hundreds of questions, it seems, for her to answer. Before this person, this test-giver, ever got here the child probably knew something was wrong with him, with her. After all, he is failing. She is not popular. Nobody likes her. He fights a lot. She is hungry. He is worried. He is afraid. They hate school.

They will not do well on a test. Something will show up that seems to say there is a problem somewhere. This would be so even if the test was a marvelous test, one that could really reach into their minds and pull out all the different kinds of knowledge that they have stored in there and that they never show anyone at all. Even if the test was that good they would not do well, because they expect to do poorly on tests. They are already failures, and this is just one more test to prove it to the world.

And the test will not be able to reach into their minds and pull out all their wonderful knowledge anyway. Many tests do not adquately test minority children, children from different cultural backgrounds, children who are not "average" kids according to someone else's idea of "average."

So all the Bens and Alices and Kits and Adams and Chucks and Lydias, in all the schools, in all the school districts, take tests and get placed in special ed. They probably did worst on the verbal parts of the test, the parts that show verbal skills. Can they read, write, understand certain vocabulary words, certain phrases? They probably did better on the performance parts of the tests, the parts that test intuitive knowledge, deductive reasoning, common sense. The intelligence, you see, is there. They may be very creative, logical, sensible, but not be able to define precise vocabulary words, particularly if they have never heard them before. They may not do well with analogies on a test, never having heard some of the terms before. They may be unfamiliar with some of the concepts presented, the terms used. It makes a difference.

The standards for placement in LD classes vary from time to time. LD has traditionally been the label given to those children who showed average or above average intelligence on IQ tests. This may mean a combined test score on both the verbal and performance tests at 78 or above, with either the verbal or performance being at least 80. More often than we think, kids who get placed in LD classes are actually gifted children. These particular gifted children became lost in a system of education that aims its products at the "average" consumer, the "average" child.

Perhaps one of them, Alice or Chuck, maybe, or even all of them, are really gifted children, children who were disabled by an inadequate education. If they are children who are more behavior problems than anything else, who wind up in BD rooms as a matter of fact, they are almost certainly there because the system couldn't handle them. More and more both LD and BD classes are being combined as a single solution to a complex problem and are being called simply LBD rooms. There may be some very gifted kids in these LBD rooms.

Ben's question at the beginning of the chapter is all the more fascinating then. How do you get a learning disability?

The Federal guidelines regulating PL94–142, the Education for All Handicapped Children Act, state:

> In order to be found learning disabled, a child must suffer from a severe discrepancy between achievement and intellectual ability in one or more of the following areas: oral expression, written expression, listening or reading comprehension, basic reading skills, mathematical calculations or reasoning, or spelling. A severe discrepancy is defined to exist when achievement in one or more of the above areas falls at or below 50% of the child's expected achievement level considering the child's age and previous educational experiences.
>
> A child may not be identified as learning disabled if his or her learning problem is primarily the result of visual, hearing, or motor handicaps, mental retardation, emotional disturbance, or environmental, cultural, or economic disadvantages; . . .[1]

How do you get LD? In their book *Teaching Children with Learning Problems,* Gerald Wallace and James Kauffman list four major areas that may be factors in the acquisition of learning disability: biophysical, sociocultural, psychodevelopmental, educational. They say:

> A child's genetic endowment and physical status obviously have a profound effect on his behavior. . . .
> Birth trauma, oxygen deprivation, infectious disease, drug intoxica-

tion, malnutrition, and congenital defects are only a few of the biological events which may influence a child's ability to learn. Attempts to pinpoint specific biological correlates of individual learning problems, however, have not been successful. . . .

. . . The social and cultural contexts in which the child lives undeniably shape his learning also. Family relationships, social class, the expectations of educational systems, and memberships in subcultural groups are known to be determining variables in the child's development. . . .

. . . There is little doubt that deteriorating family units, poverty, racial discrimination, manipulation by the media, rigid school policies, cultural fetishes and taboos, and other social and cultural factors influence the child's behavior in school. . . .

. . . Undoubtedly, anxiety about growing up, separation from one's parents, establishing one's own identity, experiencing traumatic events, learning to express one's emotions appropriately, building trusting relationships, and many other developmental and psychological processes are related to school learning. . . .

. . . It is axiomatic that learning problems may occur because of inadequate or inappropriate instruction. The child may not learn because the teacher fails to teach. . . .[2]

A child cannot be put in an LBD room because he is poor, or because she is black, or because his parents are getting a divorce, but these factors may indeed be at the roots of many a learning problem. Ben, Alice, Lydia, and the others could not become LBD because of their physical, psychological, or sociocultural problems, but these things may have influenced the kind of behaviors at school that resulted in their referral for LBD placement.

And very surely every single one of our friends could have earned their designation as LBD kids because of the final factor:

The child may not learn because the teacher fails to teach.[3]

Many different terms have been used to label kids in the past who are now simply referred to as LD or LBD kids: dyslexic, perceptually handicapped, brain-damaged, emotionally disturbed. The kids endure the labels and survive the system, somehow. More often than not, they are really "educationally deprived," victims of a shameful educational experience. The important thing is that they can come out of it still liking themselves.

The kids did an exercise one day in which they put their names in the center of a paper with Magic Markers. Then they drew lines from "themselves" to words they put down, words describing themselves, words about who they were, who they wanted to be. Here is Ben's.

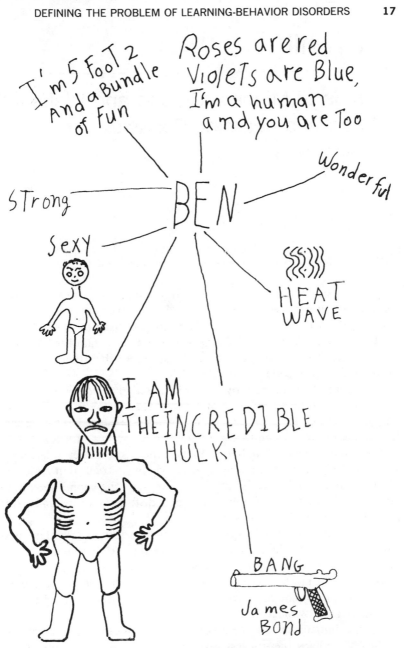

I'm 5 FooT 2 And a Bundle of Fun

Roses are red
VioleTs are Blue,
I'm a human
and you are Too

STrong — BEN — Wonderful

Sexy

HEAT WAVE

I AM THE INCREDIBLE HULK!

BANG
James Bond

Chapter III

Kids of Minority Groups and Welfare Families Learning-Behavior Disorders

CHUCK: *I don't know. It started when you was born, I guess.*

"My children will never be bused. They will never go to school with those immoral children."

"Why don't they ship all those damn niggers back to Africa?"

"I've done my part for civil rights. I've got three families of 'them' living on my block. I don't have to do any more than that. I will not let my child go to school with 'them.'"

These remarks were made by three white mothers who voiced publicly what so many others think and feel but would not say in public. They continue racism. They preserve and persevere in hatred. They ensure that there will always be inequality and, thus, victims of inequality.

The "immoral children," the "them," the niggers they referred to were all blacks, but there are many other victims of racism in America.

The man who tells his family, his children, at the supper table that "they ought to let those damn boat people drift away to sea and never pick them up" is also a racist.

The woman who stands up on a nationally televised talk show and tells the world that she doesn't want any of those Cambodian refugees moving into her neighborhood is continuing the racism.

The family—mother, father, children—who terrorize a Vietnamese family, forcing them to move from a low-rent housing project, are practicing racial violence.

All the Indians on all the reservations in this whole country are victims of perhaps the cruelest racist policies of all. Their culture has

18

been very nearly destroyed. They have been reduced from proud peoples to beggars.

The Mexicans, the Haitians, the Puerto Ricans, the Cubans have all felt the effects of racism in the United States of America. There is always the wish to "drive them out," make them "illegal aliens," send them back where they came from.

This hatred, this fear, this racism has gone on for hundreds of years. It is generations old. It is an ancient malady, a sickness that creeps from one generation to the next and infects the young almost as soon as they are aware of life. It follows the young to school.

When a child has a teacher who cannot bring herself to touch black children, that child suffers a hurt, a trauma.

When a child, standing with his father in the school office, hears two of his teachers say as they pass him, "What can you expect of him—his father's a nigger and his mother's white?", that child will be traumatized by the violence of racism.

When a child has a teacher who, every night, "airs" her clothes to get the "nigger smell" out of them, the effects of racism cannot do anything else but hurt him every single school day.

It does not take long for a learning disability or a behavior problem to develop. It can start as soon as a child perceives his rejection by the teacher. It can start as soon as the child realizes she is different, and somehow inferior, as far as her treatment by others is concerned. It can start as soon as a child is born, when there have been years of telling a group of people that they are subhuman, inferior, illegal, immoral, trash.

If the child perceives that there are many people out there who would really prefer it if he were invisible, gone from the face of the earth, banished, nonexistent, he will develop his own ways of dealing with that hate. If the child senses that certain people are confused by her presence, fear her, resent her intrusion, she will learn to cope with the problem as best she can. Because the child is in such a vulnerable situation, being a small human being in a big school system, the pressures of the violent attitudes, even where the violence is repressed, are enough to create serious school problems.

There is the hurt of the little girl, a black girl, who was the only girl not invited to a birthday party in the "other" neighborhood.

There is the awareness expressed by the children at play, when they answer the child who says she wants to marry Charlie Brown when she grows up with, "You can't marry Charlie Brown. He's white."

There is the frustration, intense, hostile, desperate, expressed by the mother to her child at a school conference, "Just do what they tell you in this white-ass school. They don't care about you."

The children bring their lives, their whole lives, with them to school each morning. They do not come with a "clean slate" every day, with all the experiences of yesterday and all the yesterdays before that wiped off for a fresh new start on a fresh new day. No, they sit down each morning and all the evil, all the meanness, all the garbage that has been dumped on them for a lifetime crashes down into their seats with them. They can't get away from their lives, who they are, how other people treat them. They use up a lot of energy just getting to school, what with all that load on them. Sometimes any energy that's left over gets put into playing all day at school. Why not? That may seem to be the best solution. At least make a game of this mess. Sometimes the energy is all used up and there is not any left over for learning to read.

And this is how it happens that many minority children get put in LBD classes. The children fall behind or become problems to someone and get referred to LBD.

These are the children of all those races, all those peoples, who are continually deprived of a full share of a birthright as human beings in this country, who need to turn to violence from time to time just to attract someone's attention to their misery, to the injustice being done to them. These are the children of those people who have never been treated as fully equal in this country, whose cultures have been suppressed or destroyed, whose rage at their contemptuous treatment by other Americans sometimes explodes in desperate, hopeless, futile destruction.

"Those niggers tear down everything they have, don't they?" said the young girl on her first visit to the inner city.

"Those damn Indians are too damned lazy to even mine the gold in these hills," said the old prospector about the land that rightfully belonged to the Sioux but which the government had taken from them.

"My daddy says thank God that nigger's dead," said the fifth grader upon the death of Martin Luther King.

For the children of these minority races it would be a very easy thing to become LBD. It is, perhaps, a disease that infects the ghettos.

There are other diseases that infect the ghetto. There are other factors in the inner cities, or the small towns, or the farmlands that cause LBD problems. One of these factors is poverty.

Poverty may affect any race, any group of people. There are people from all races, in all parts of the country, on welfare. Welfare keeps people from starving to death, but it may also promote the kind of spiritual decay that destroys the will for a full life, for achievement, for growth.

Many children come from homes where the monthly check for Aid to Dependent Children is the expected allotment for life, where all food is purchased with food stamps, and all medical care is "purchased" with a medical card. These children are usually on free lunches at school. They cannot buy their school pictures unless the "check" comes on time. They often don't have money for field trips. Their clothes usually come from secondhand stores. They get cheap haircuts. They have their own value system.

Many of these children will leave school early to get jobs, to join the service, to drift on the streets. While they are in school, they are disinterested, unchallenged, bored. There is nothing in school that makes any difference to them, so they think, and they often develop their own programs of failure. They are "dropouts" who just haven't taken the final step out the door yet. They are absent even when they are present, and they are not present very much.

One child stayed home to play cards with her mother and watch TV all day, most days. She transferred from school to school in the course of a year and managed to evade the authorities enough to skip school for about two-thirds of every year. In seventh grade she could not read words from a first-grade book. "I really tricked those schools," she said. "They thought I was sick all that time. I won a game on them."

Another mother kept her nine children home from school occasionally for lessons of her own. She locked the doors, drew the blinds, and paired off her children. They fought each other till there was a final winner. This was so nobody would take advantage of her children.

Two boys cut classes to get high. They burned a neighbor's house down and stabbed the small dog to death.

The purpose of education is to help people to make choices and to cope with change. When there is no hope for change, when no choices are available, then the education is meaningless.

That there is very little hope for change or choices available is obvious to the young mother who is going back to school to become a Licensed Practical Nurse. She receives an additional check for school costs now. This check is for $144. Out of this she pays $120 to put her small daughter in a nursery school while she attends classes. Her rent has gone from $60 to $80 because she is getting this new check, and her food-stamp allotment has been reduced from $115 to $56. She is actually being penalized financially in the attempt to better herself and get off welfare.

For many the choice has been simple. It is easier to stay on welfare than to fight the system. There are many children who come from families that have been on welfare for two or three generations. They know no other way of life, and for many the penalties are too high to attempt to get off the welfare system.

The children of these families are doomed from the start. They show no interest in a system of education that rewards those who "get ahead," who do better than others on test scores, in classwork, in competition. They are not interested in competing in a system that seems bent on "keeping them in their place." They see nothing in it for themselves in trying to excel in school. They are simply "turned off" to the educational system. They fail often. They grow up as failures. Some are failures before they ever get started.

He was the second of three children to the nineteen-year-old welfare mother. He told the visitor he went to nursery school and that he was "in the slow toddler class." He was four years old.

Another little boy was picked up by the police for breaking and entering when he was five years old. He had been caught stealing food out of a neighbor's refrigerator.

The little three-year-old girl and her four-year-old brother sat close to their mother on the sofa in the hot upstairs room that smelled of cat litter, where the cats climbed all over the backs of chairs, the table tops, everything. The children clung to the woman. They had not learned to talk yet and made baby sounds for all their communication.

Many of the welfare children are foster children, whose lives are already so traumatized that education, school, is just one more hurdle to overcome. They have been disconnected from all that made sense of their existences, their own homes, and school becomes one more area of confusion. School may provide a very real focal point for them to vent their rage. Or they may withdraw from the primary activity of school, namely learning, in their bewilderment.

One little girl systematically fed peanut butter to the fish in the fish tank at her foster mother's house, because peanut butter was almost all she got to eat, and she knew that most of the check for her went to build up this fish tank.

An eleven-year-old boy had already been in sixteen foster homes. He messed in his pants every day at school and hid them in his locker.

These children become old early. They have sex early and children soon. They get caught up in the old, old problems and can't get out.

The young man is extremely intelligent. He has a good friend who wants to help him get straightened out. The friend even takes him along when he moves to another city. The young man's girlfriend calls him two, three, or four times a day. She wants him home. She needs him. They have two children. What can she do by herself? They are both held down by the same crushing load. They are poor. They have no skills. They don't know how to get out from under this burden.

It is the sense of hopelessness that so defeats these kids when they are in school. They do not believe that things can ever be any different, and they are afraid to try. They pursue the courses they have always known, and these usually lead to failure. And, often, to referrals for special ed., to LBD rooms.

There is a nursery rhyme that goes:

As I walked by myself
And talked to myself,
Myself said unto me:
"Look to thyself,
Take care of thyself,
For nobody cares for thee."

I answered myself
And said to myself
In the selfsame repartee:
"Look to thyself
Or not look to thyself,
The selfsame thing will be."
                              —Myself[4]

These are some examples of problems in the sociocultural area that seriously affect some children's performance at school. The Federal law requires that children not be put in special ed. rooms just because they are poor or come from minority situations. However, those very factors play an important part in influencing the kinds of work certain children do in school.

The CBS program *60 Minutes* did a segment in the fall of 1979 on a lovely South Pacific island that the United States had turned into a welfare state. It had once been self-sufficient, with a perfectly balanced ecology and useful work for everyone. Now the ecology was upset, the elderly were wasting away in old people's homes, and they were planning on starting some special ed. units. "What if," the reporter asked the new special ed. teacher from the states, "you can't find any children for these classes?" "Oh, we'll find them," she replied, "we have to find them."

Children can be referred to LBD classes for other reasons. Some children suffer from actual birth-related defects that have made it impossible for them to function successfully in regular class programs. Others have suffered infections that have impaired the normal functioning of the brain. Poor diet may be a cause of learning problems. These factors are more difficult to ascertain in some instances, as the technology is not there to make accurate decisions about the extent and kind of damage that exists. However, there are children who experience a kind of "block" that impedes the learning process.

The "blocks" that other children suffer because of emotional hurts are varied. Obviously, any child who is a victim of prejudice suffers emotional trauma. Children from poverty areas may very likely be emotionally deprived also, simply as a consequence of the economic doldrums of their everyday existences. But there are children from homes, the so-called "normal" American homes, who suffer from abuse, verbal, emotional, or physical, and who become candidates for LBD classes. Emotional factors are hard to discover in most cases. One just finds so many kids who can't keep up in school, who don't perform up to the expectations for the "normal" child.

And again, there will be the children who are in special ed. because of the failure of schools to teach.

As you can see, though, Chuck was right when he assumed that, in many cases, you got LD when you were born. Here is Chuck's analysis of himself.

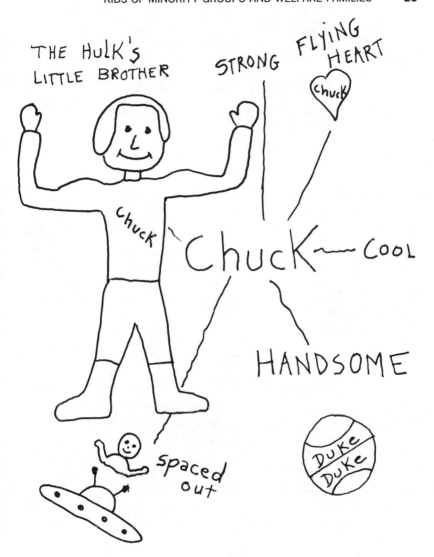

Chapter IV

The Schools and Learning-
Behavior Disorder Problems

ADAM: *I got it when I was in first grade.*

At the beginning of this book, I told you about an exercise we were
doing in class that had to do with a very special book. That book is
Richard DeMille's *Put Your Mother on the Ceiling*. The exercise in
the book that the class liked best is the one that DeMille calls "Breath-
ing." This is part of it:

> Breathe in some fire./ Have it burning
> and crackling in your chest./ Breathe it
> out again./ Breathe in some logs of
> wood./ Set fire to them in your chest./
> Have them roaring as they burn up./
> Breathe out the smoke and ashes./
>
> Have a big tree in front of you./
> Breathe fire on the tree and burn it
> all up./ Have an old castle in front of
> you./ Breathe fire on the castle and
> have it fall down./ Have an ocean in
> front of you./ Breathe fire on the
> ocean and dry it up./
>
> What would you like to breathe in now?/
> All right./ What would you like to burn
> up by breathing fire on it?/ All right./[5]

They do this exercise when they are quiet, peaceful, calm. They close their eyes and try to bring the images before them. They take in deep breaths and imagine the fire rolling around inside their throats, inside their lungs, deep down inside themselves. Then they breathe out all the fire and "destroy" the things that bug them.

For a long time into the school year, these kids want to destroy words, and school, and their teachers. They would like to attack all the words, all the schools, and all the teachers. They want to attack them, slay them, disarm them so that these almighty forces in their lives will feel the full effects of their power and surrender to them.

Kids are powerless in school. They are manipulated by many different forces that seem to operate in isolation from them and from their needs.

One of the key forces that tend to isolate them is the syllabus, the course of studies, the curriculum. The curriculum is written for the average child. It outlines, say, what the average fourth grader ought to be able to digest about Japan, or about the Iroquois Indians, or about long division. It is usually written by teachers who want to make some extra money in the summertime. It is an aid to teachers, listing reference guides for them, and providing ideas for activities. It is a very straightforward document, concise and pertinent. It is also very rigid. In focusing attention on the subject matter to be learned by the "average child," it ignores the entire educational challenge of teaching the gifted child, the educationally deprived child. The assumption is that in providing for a wide range of activities, all these "other" children will be reached, brought under the umbrella with the average learner. That assumption is based on the philosophy that indeed that is where every child should be, under the umbrella with the average learner. The idea is that if enough gimmicks are used, enough learning centers, or enough "creative" ways of presenting the material, all children in a class will reach the same goal. Eventually they will all master the material with the expected percent of accuracy. They will all, in time, realize the same objective, the mastery of the information as the curriculum outlines it.

The curriculum itself can provide the teachers with a lot of headaches. There are teachers, for instance, who are presented with a curriculum guide that requires the children to use a certain textbook in order to fulfill the requirements of that curriculum for that year. Yet, the State Department of Education decides to "adopt," or purchase, an entirely different set of textbooks for that class. The teacher then has to have books of both sets handy for herself/himself. The teacher has to be able to find all the specific information needed for a subject from the "recommended" text, yet use the "adopted" text with the children. In some states the students are given periodic tests based on the material outlined in the curriculum. These tests may come from the State Department of Education.

The regular classroom teachers are part of the problem, a large part of it, for the "nonaverage" child. The nonaverage children, whether these be gifted learners or "slow" learners, make their jobs harder. Even though many of them have attended workshops in recent years on how to present the material in more diverse ways, they would really prefer to have their average children in a neat, tight little classroom. They may have learned a great deal about individualization and learning packets and modules for individualized learning, but it is, by and large, a pain in the neck to most teachers to have to go to all this trouble. Especially to have to go to all this trouble when there are LBD teachers or "gifted" teachers right there in the building who could, who *should,* take these kids off their hands full time. They have a lot of resentment for both the kids and the teachers from the "pull-out" or PT (part-time) programs.

When it seemed that Chuck could handle the regular reading class for one hour a day, I conferred with his teacher and sent him. He was, after all, reading at or above the level of her children by this time. He was also wiry, overactive, full of mischief. The very next day Chuck came back to my class with a note: "Chuck is not ready for us and we are not ready for him."

There was the regular program teacher who, on the second day of school, informed the LBD teacher that if a certain LBD child stayed in her room for any classes that year, she was going to fail him.

Regular program teachers require LBD kids (and gifted kids) to make up any and all work they miss from their classes while they are in their part-time rooms. Thus, a child who has assignments to do for the special classes must make up work from the regular programs. These children are penalized for being "special," whether gifted or LBD. They have twice the work, sometimes, that the average kids have. And there are teachers who have attempted to fail these children when they got so far behind that they couldn't possibly make up all their assignments.

LBD teachers learn to dodge the other teachers, avoid the teachers' lounge. The regular program teachers resent it that special ed. teachers are limited to a certain number of children per class when their own rooms are overcrowded. They feel that if a child has been admitted to a special program, the burden of educating that child ought to be removed from them entirely.

One regular class teacher who had managed to avoid taking any special ed. students for two years asked in a faculty meeting why they had to take more of these kids in their rooms than the special ed. teachers were required to take. In other words, if an LBD teacher only had to take eight children in a class, why were there sometimes more than eight LBD kids in a regular teacher's room?

Another regular program teacher stated on the third day of school that there was going to be war between the regular program staff and the special ed. staff before the year was over.

A regular program teacher failed a child. This happened after weekly meetings and reports to the special ed. teacher on this child, at which the child's progress was continuously noted as very satisfactory. The principal upheld the decision, saying it would be a good learning experience for the child. This child had only gained the full use of speech two years before this occurrence. He was in eighth grade at the time. He was LD.

The regular program staff are angry and resentful whenever they are asked to keep their special ed. kids in their classes for a day or two. They let the special ed. teachers know about it.

The *MacNeil/Lehrer Report* did a program on teacher burn-out in June, 1980. One of the major grievances of the teacher on the broadcast was the fact that teachers have to deal with so many special ed. kids in their rooms. She expressed a great deal of bitterness over this issue.

However, this was never an "issue" until a few years ago, until the Federal government passed a law called the Education for All Handicapped Children Act, or, as it is better known, PL94–142. Until so much attention was given to the "cause" of handicapped children, the children who are now labeled LBD were probably integrated into regular programs. Now that their "problem" status has been authenticated by a team of experts, the LBD kids are resented in the mainstream classes. Teachers are determined to get a classroom full of "average" kids.

Many children who are in LBD are, or were, average kids at one time. They may simply have gone about the process of learning a little bit differently than some of their classmates. Or they may not have been given the attention they needed. Our friend Ben recognized that fact. He knew that if he raised his hand he would be ignored. There are other children who haven't been able to hear the teacher from where they sat, or couldn't see the board from their seats, or who didn't understand the assignment. They get behind. The distance between them and their classmates grows, the pressure to keep up accumulates, and they get to a point where they cannot manage the pace. If they had been in a system that treated them as individuals instead of demanding of them an "average" performance, they might have been quite successful in their school lives.

There are those children who are "perceptually handicapped," who have difficulty with the symbols and sounds of reading, the symbols of math. There are those children for whom it is a problem to put things in sequence, or who cannot remember the direction in which words and phrases are read. There are children who make reversals in handwriting or with numbers, or who cannot grasp a pencil and make legible, decipherable symbols on paper.

There are those children who might be called "dyslexic," or brain-damaged, or neurologically impaired. They may be very uncoordinated. They may have very little eye control. They may resemble traffic lights that have gone out of whack. The flow and control of traffic is done by means of a sophisticated technology that "sees" and "counts" the amount of traffic and changes the lights in order to keep the flow constant. It controls the incoming information and determines the kind of output necessary to keep cars running through smoothly. When there is a breakdown in the system, either the incoming information isn't being processed correctly or the mechanisms that control output are faulty. This is something like what happens in a child who really can't coordinate sensory information, the knowledge acquired by touch, taste, sound, smell, with the way he or she acts or learns. What goes in doesn't make sense with what comes out by way of answers, responses, behavior. Somewhere the computer, which is the brain, seems not to be functioning properly. There are children like this who show up in the schools, in the regular classes.

Even more of these children might be able to remain in regular programs if those programs were not so rigidly geared toward the "average" child. And there is more and more evidence that many gifted children are actually in LBD rooms. These gifted children were misjudged, overlooked, poorly taught. Someone, or a lot of someones, confused their actual genius with recalcitrance, or strangeness, or peculiarity. They wound up in LBD rooms, probably labeled "retarded," obstinate, unruly, or withdrawn by the diagnostic team after consultation with the staff.

Many children become special ed. kids in the teachers' lounge. Kids have been destroyed for life in teachers' lounges. Personal information

2. I am the smartest kid

about children is often shared there. A lot of complaining goes on there, and it is often about kids, particular kids. A child's "case" may become the topic of a day's discussion, at the end of which the consensus seems to be that the child's teacher ought really to refer him or her for LBD.

There is a nursery rhyme called Jack Jelf. It goes:

> Little Jack Jelf
> Was put on the shelf
> Because he could not spell "pie."
> When his aunt, Mrs. Grace,

Saw his sorrowful face,
She could not help saying, "Oh fie!"
And since Master Jelf
Was put on the shelf
Because he could not spell "pie,"
Let him stand there so grim,
And no more about him,
For I wish him a very good-bye![6]

"The child may not learn because the teacher fails to teach."[7]

There was the mother who came to school in tears because her child had been cutting class for weeks and was failing and no one had told her. "Why?" she demanded of the teacher, "why didn't you tell me this was going on?"

"She hadn't killed anybody yet," was the teacher's reply.

A little boy's father came and begged all his child's teachers, the principal, the counselor to help him help his son. The boy was getting bad conduct grades. Yet every teacher present said the boy behaved well in her class. It was in the halls that the child acted up, and this is what he was marked for on the report card. In that particular school there was no discipline in the halls; there was general chaos in the halls; there was never any quiet in the halls. There was no control in the school, and this child received bad conduct grades for a problem beyond his control.

There was the mother who came to see the teacher about her little boy. She was crying. He had failed and was being referred to LBD. But she had told the teacher he had trouble seeing the board, and all the spelling words were on the board. Why hadn't the teacher moved him so he could see the board?

"Oh," said the teacher. She hadn't remembered.

And more deadly than even these examples is the daily routine of attempting to treat each and every child in a class as an average child. There is the day-after-day grinding struggle to get all kids in a class to conform to a mold, to learn that curriculum, to achieve a predetermined level of mastery on tests. Those who don't make it fail or are sent to special ed.

This is Lydia's perception of herself shortly after she entered the LBD class. The little figures on the bottom are either ghosts or tombstones. I think.

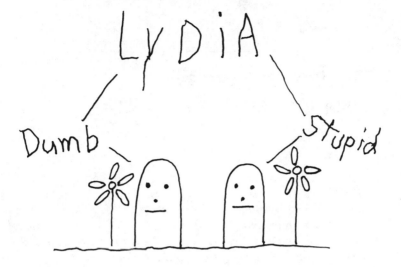

Chapter V

The Learning-Behavior Disorder Class

ALICE: *You get behind, so when you go to LD they try to get you up to your grade. If you get good grades long enough, they probably try you out in the regular classes again.*

BEN: *Then if you start dropping back down, you come in here again.*

In 1975 the Federal government passed PL94–142, the Education for All Handicapped Children Act. Since the passage of that law, all the public schools in the country have had to develop programs and policies to provide the education for handicapped children that they require. There are many guidelines to follow. There is a lot of Federal money given to the states to help them implement the law and provide the services these children need. There are hundreds of forms to fill out to show that the correct procedures are being followed in regard to every child referred to or diagnosed for a special program.

One of the provisions stipulates that each special ed. child be given an individualized educational program every year that the child is in the special class. This program should outline in detail what the educational or behavioral goals are for that child, the materials that will be used in the process of remediation, and the testing that will be done to determine the effectiveness of the strategies, and the program should be signed by everyone concerned with the education of the child: parents, teachers, counselors, principal.

At least once during each school year, the parents of the special ed. child are to be invited to the school for a conference with all the child's teachers and the administrative staff. The child may come to this conference also. The child should have the right to express feelings and views about the program. The parents must sign the forms that outline their child's program for the coming year. This is their consent for special services to be given and their agreement with the type of education, the methods, their child will be exposed to. The parents may come to school for visits many more times than that. Both the parents and the children are protected by the law. They have certain rights, may make certain demands to ensure the best education available for the children.

The goal is for children to be able to improve their skills, both behaviorally and academically, so that they may return to more normal educational programs in regular classes. While in special ed., each child is to be placed in the "least restrictive environment" according to his or her needs and capabilities. If a child has the ability to take part in some of the classes that his or her classmates in the regular program do, then this child may not be kept in an LBD class all day. A self-contained program is one in which certain children remain in the special ed. room all day because their behavior or academic level of performance warrants their absolute separation from regular classes. Most times, LBD children are placed in "resource rooms," where they spend only a portion of each day in LBD working on specific areas that need strengthening. These children are said to be "mainstreamed" for whatever part of the day that they return to regular programs. The goal is to help LBD children improve their skills, their level of functioning both academically and behaviorally, so that eventually they may get out of special ed. They then would be fully "mainstreamed."

It becomes a recycling process. The effects of this recycling on the children are often very damaging. When the children feel unwanted in the regular programs and know that the regular program teachers have the leverage to "get them out" of those classes and back into LBD, the children lose hope, lose trust. The teachers, also, become confused and irritated. They feel they are caught, unfairly, in the middle of this recycling process and that the constant flow of LBD children in and out of their rooms has made life harder for them than it was before the law. They often become bitter.

One regular program teacher recounted all her efforts to help a child. She told the others at the child's conference, the parents, the LBD teachers, the counselor, and the principal, "But I can do only so much. I have too many students. They all have problems. I am only one person, and I'm not superhuman." She experienced much the same frustration expressed by the teacher on the *MacNeil/Lehrer Report* in June, 1980. This is one of the factors of teacher burn-out for regular program teachers.

But teacher burn-out is a significant problem for special ed. teachers, too. The burn-out rate for special ed. teachers is three years. Special ed. teachers become burned out much sooner than do regular program teachers.

There is a television commercial that shows a teacher sitting alone with a child, reading with him. Someone says, "If a rock star can earn a million dollars by giving a concert, why isn't it worth as much to teach a child to read?"

The financial rewards of teaching the handicapped learners are not commensurate with the demands of the job. Beginning teachers, depending on the state in which they teach, probably make from $10,000 to $15,000 a year. Twenty-five years later, if they stay in it that long, they an expect to make probably only twice their starting salary. It is not unusual for a teacher to be making between $20,000 and $25,000 after twenty-five years of teaching disabled learners and behaviorally disordered children.

Very few men are in the field of special ed. It is an extremely demanding, draining job, with few financial rewards and little hope of advancement.

The financial rewards are poor for special ed. teachers, as they are for all the other teachers. But special ed. teachers see very little progress in their students, very little return for all their work. The older the children are in the LBD room, the less progress is usually apparent. A child may have come into the LBD program in a certain grade, say, eighth grade, reading at a fourth-grade level. That means the child had accomplished only one-half year of reading for every year in school. If the LBD teacher manages to help that child raise the level of reading so that going into ninth grade he or she has improved by a whole year, that may be a 100 percent gain over the previous year, but the child is still only reading at a fifth-grade level in the ninth grade. It becomes very discouraging. In order to achieve that 100 percent increase in the achievement level, the teacher had to do an awful lot of things right and be blessed with an extraordinary amount of luck besides. Just as friction reduces the speed of an accelerating object, many factors have the same effect on learning for the LBD child. There are psychological factors impinging on the LBD child. He/she hates to be in that

LBD room. The older the child, the more intense is the shame, the hatred of being thus singled out. There are physical factors. The child may be having a bad day every so often. The physical factors of the overall school plant need to be taken into account here. If there is no discipline in a school, the LBD child will return from the lunchroom in a state of frenzy. Or the experience of going through the halls will

4. School is like a yellow balloon

be a catastrophic one. The rest of the day may be "shot" for the LBD teacher as well as for the child. There is often just plain discouragement for the LBD child. Then he or she may stay home, cut classes, get into trouble, be suspended.

When one considers that a 100 percent improvement doesn't amount to a significant change in an LBD child's life, it is little wonder that the LBD teacher becomes frustrated. After all, a ninth grader reading on a fifth-grade level, although not as disadvantaged as the eighth grader reading on a fourth-grade level, still has to remain in special programs for more help. There seems to be no end to the problem of remediation.

The LBD teacher may go home each night so tired, so discouraged, so frustrated that she or he has little energy for anything else. This teacher, far more than any other teacher in a building, will tend to become absorbed in the problems her/his students face. This teacher, more than any other teacher in a building, will be sapped of energy in the attempt to bring students up to a level where they can return to regular programs. This would amount to the incredible task, say, where the teacher deals with fifteen students a day, of providing such individualized instruction for fifteen children, all on different levels of achievement, that those children could make the 200 percent or 300 percent or 400 percent gains in achievement needed to return them to regular classes.

Then, too, there is the fact that not all these children need just reading help. Some may not need reading help at all. There are those who require math remediation. There are those who need to learn to write, or to spell. Many need help in all areas. Some just need to learn how to accomplish tasks accurately, how to follow directions, how to study. Some children need to learn how to listen.

There are those children who need the teacher's hand to guide them through each step of making a letter. There are those children who forget overnight the steps to solving a long-division problem. There are those children who cannot work unless the teacher sits right with them, encouraging them every step of the way.

One LBD teacher complained that she had thought, on a day when several of her students were absent, that it would be an easy day. On the contrary, just that much more energy needed to be put in the programs, the individualized instruction, of the others. She had still gone home exhausted.

The LBD teacher may decide to put the behaviorally disordered kids on a system of behavior modification to help them adjust better to their school environment. There may be unexpected eruptions of problem behavior from time to time. Some days the kids, all of them or some of them, may decide that they just don't want to learn anything that day. The kids who come into the room in the afternoon may be too exhausted to do anything more of value for the rest of the day.

The LBD teacher may get complaints from regular program teachers every day. The LBD teacher may know that his/her students are being treated unfairly in certain regular classes in a school and may not be able to do anything about it. The LBD teacher may have a very unsympathetic principal, a school counselor who is too busy or who thinks that the LBD teacher should handle all his/her own problems.

Parents may be angry in general at a school or at the "system" and take out their frustration on the LBD teacher. After all, this is the person who works most closely with their child. Or parents may try to "cover" for their children.

A parent says, "Why can't you control him at school? He never talks back to me?" In the background of this phone conversation, the boy can be heard calling his mother names.

Or another parent says, "I take care of my child at home. I expect you to discipline her at school. That's your problem."

There is the parent who said about her child who was not improving, "Just fail him, that's all. Go ahead and fail him."

There was the parent who reacted in anger at a conference called about her son's increasing behavior problems. The LBD teacher told the parent there was reason to believe, although it couldn't be proved, that her son was involved in taking drugs, distributing them to others. The point was made that this was a suspicion, nothing more, but that it was pretty well founded. The parent was furious that anyone would say such a thing about her son.

"I think that's terrible that you would say such a thing without proof," she said.

It was later discovered that the boy was never at home from the time he got off his school bus until 10:00 or 10:30 at night. He came home from school, ate a sandwich, rode his bike to a nearby shopping center and played in the "game" rooms there until bedtime.

An LBD teacher ought to be pleased and proud when a student makes a 100 percent gain in the LBD class. But so much more needs to be done and the whole effort seems so frustrating, so futile, at times, that the LBD teacher is a good candidate for burn-out after only three years at this job.

There is, after all, all that friction reducing the acceleration speed of the LBD teacher's efforts. There are the children themselves, and the parents who never even bother to come for the yearly conferences, the hostile co-workers, occasionally the unsympathetic principal. There is the factor of all the paperwork that has to be done on each child to satisfy the government regulations. And there is the dismal prospect of earning anything near the value, the very real value, of the effort the teacher puts forth, of the results achieved.

A teacher in an **LBD** room takes comfort from what small things are available, such as Adam's appraisal of himself. Not a small thing, after all.

Chapter VI

Becoming a Learning-
Behavior Disorders Teacher

ADAM: *I feel like the teacher doesn't lie to me in LD.*

The Clock

There's a neat little clock—
In the schoolroom it stands—
And it points to the time
With its two little hands.

And may we, like the clock,
Keep a face clean and bright,
With hands ever ready
To do what is right.[8]

What kind of person is the LBD teacher?

To be able to work with her students so that she can help them the most, she must have some very feminine qualities. She must be warm, loving, tender, soft, touching, and vulnerable. She must be able to laugh readily and cry easily. She ought not be a perfectionist, because she is being given the job of working with some very imperfect others, children with problems. She must be the kind of person who can reach out and touch others often and who does not draw back when they touch her. She must be able to stifle her feelings of disgust when some children are dirty, or smell, or have runny noses. She has to be kind even to the child who bites her or who threatens to jump out the window whenever things get tough. She ought to have a soft voice and use it lovingly. She ought not to be cruel, the kind of person who, in desperation sometimes, says terrible things to children to get them under control or to make them work. She ought to be strong, so strong that she can keep coming back to that classroom day after day, even though she may have cried all night because there is so much to do, and the children don't seem ready *ever* to return to regular programs, and other staff members snub her and talk about her children, and she loves those children so much.

I have used the feminine pronoun throughout that description. There certainly are some men who become special ed. teachers, not very many, but some. It is still a touchy subject, a shameful kind of thing, to say, in our culture anyway, that a man can have a feminine side to his nature. It is precisely this feminine side, the soft, gentle, caring side of a man's nature that best fits him to be a special ed. teacher. This is the side of him that is creative and nurturing and understanding. There is great need for more men in the field of special ed., more men who feel sure enough about themselves that they can risk being tender and pliable without feeling a threat to their idea of themselves as men.

The special ed. teacher has to be someone who can encourage without driving children. The special ed. teacher has to be able to accept lots of disappointments and defeats. When the child that you've sent back to the regular teacher throws a tantrum or runs out of the school and heads for home, the sense of failure is acute. When it's always, always, always *your* kids who get in trouble anywhere in the school, and you feel so responsible for them every minute of the day, no matter where they are, and you feel like a pariah for being *that* teacher with *those* kids, the pressure gets to be enormous. The special ed. teacher has to be able to accept the kids' failures without assuming that burden of failure as his or her own defeat. There has to be a sense of separateness from the kids. Their problems cannot become the problems of the special ed. teacher, no matter how much the rest of the staff tries to dump those problems on the special ed. teacher. The problems of the kids cannot become the problems of the special ed. teacher if the teacher is to help the kids. And, as far as the rest of the staff is concerned, they very well may be responsible for a large share of the problems many of the kids exhibit.

To be able to work with the staff, the special ed. teacher needs to be something like an artist on the high wire of the circus. If the special ed. teacher avoids the teachers' lounge, he or she will be classified as a snob. However, to frequent the teachers' lounge may be an exercise in masochism. There are days when all talking stops when the LBD teacher enters the lounge. What were they talking about? There are days when the full attack comes on and everyone "gangs up," so to speak, complaining about the children, always complaining about the

5. Field trip

children in LBD. The teachers want to know why they have to put up with these kids at all; why does there have to be mainstreaming; why does the LBD teacher have so few kids and they have overflowing classes? It is very difficult for the special ed. teacher, who needs to be a more sensitive, loving person in order to handle the job of LBD, not to identify with the children and feel a personal attack in these circumstances.

This is a very real problem, the animosity between regular staff and special ed. teachers. Entire workshops on in-service days have sometimes deteriorated into raging verbal conflicts between the groups. Panel discussions planned for the express purpose of allowing, encouraging open and frank communication between special ed. teachers and their counterparts in the regular program have often ended in increased bitterness on both sides. There are supervisors who tell their special ed. teachers to avoid the teachers' lounge as much as possible, because most other staff people think special ed. teachers have an easy enough time of it as it is. They ought, in other words, to be in their rooms planning, working. There are those experts, on the other hand, who advise special ed. teachers to go into the lounge, become visible, be a dynamic part of the whole staff. You will have to decide for yourself.

To get along with the administration, the principal, supervisors, and counselors, the LBD teacher needs to be an organization person. Not too many innovative, daring ideas ought to be demonstrated in the classroom. The LBD teacher, like every other teacher, ought to be pretty much of a yes man or woman at least until the three or four years leading to tenure status are over. That is the way the system works. Administrators like smooth sailing, with as few headaches from staff as possible. Administrators like teachers with good discipline, teachers who can handle the bulk of their problems themselves, and who don't send kids to the office every time they need correction. Particularly in regard to the LBD classes will this be so. The principal, as does everyone else, figures the very presence of the LBD class in the building means that there is another expert here, the LBD teacher, who has the unique job of dealing with certain problems and of relieving others of those burdens. At times a principal may request a teacher to take more than the allowable number of children into an LBD room or to take other duties in the building that might conflict with the teacher's performance of duties as an LBD teacher. This doesn't happen often, but the fact is that the principal is far more sympathetic with and concerned for the regular program teachers, who seem to bear so much greater a share of the burden in helping that principal run the school. The principal probably came up through the ranks anyway, having gone into administrative work after having been a regular classroom teacher. So the problems, the crises, the urgencies of the regular classroom will be far more familiar to such a principal. However, every principal knows the Federal law regarding education for the handicapped and is well aware of all the stipulations of that law as they affect a particular situation. The LBD teacher is protected by the

Federal law. The LBD teacher has the Federal law to rely on if the need ever arises. Some teachers feel the need to volunteer for extra-duty kinds of things, like sponsoring the cheerleaders or monitoring the cafeteria during breakfast just to show good will, or school spirit, or a feel for the general welfare of the place. It is a difficult task to be a good LBD teacher and to win the admiration and respect of all the staff just for what one is, an LBD teacher.

It requires a great deal of diplomacy to deal with the parents of LBD children. Often these parents feel guilty that their child is having such problems and is so far behind. They may feel it is due to something that happened in the home. Maybe they were too hard on the child, causing the child to feel inferior, to respond to the world negatively. Maybe they were incapable of demonstrating their love, and so the child withdrew into a shell. Maybe they spoiled their child, and now the child will not take any outside direction and has no self-control either. Maybe it happened at birth, or before birth during the pregnancy, or before that even, in the very genetic structure of the parents, or of one of them. Which one? It is very frightening and threatening for parents to feel that possibly one of them, the self, is responsible for such trauma in a loved child's life. They often get very defensive in dealing with school staff about their "problem" children. They feel, especially at conferences when they are surrounded by so many of the staff, that these "experts" are here to tell them what they don't want to hear. They feel that these "experts" can see right through them, put their feelers out and perceive the whole problem, and that they find them, the parents, guilty. They may, therefore, act very hostile to the teachers. They may cry. They may hide facts that would help the teachers if the facts were known. They may resent the whole process and never come in for conferences. Somehow they know their child will get better help in LBD so they sign the papers, but they never come in. Occasionally there will be the parent who wants a child in LBD, a child who does not need to be there, who is performing satisfactorily in the regular program. Somehow, this parent reasons, the child will get more attention in LBD and make more progress there.

Workshops are often held for parents of special ed. children to acquaint them with all the aspects of the Federal law and the rights both they and their children have under the law. A national organization, the Association for Children with Learning Disabilities, puts out a publication called "Closer Look" for the parents of special ed. children.

The ACLD has chapters in cities and towns throughout the country. It is an extremely valuable experience for the teachers of LBD children to belong to such an organization, to get better acquainted with the parents of LBD kids. These parents suffer great pain because of their children's problems in school. They cry sometimes. They cry in public. They don't understand why this has all happened, or where they fit in, or who is to blame. They just want the best possible education for their children. They come to see the LBD teacher as the only friend their children, and they, have.

Other advocacy groups for students and parents of special ed. students are being formed all over the country. Parents are becoming more aware of their rights as parents of special ed. kids and are becoming more active. They know they can appeal decisions made about putting their children in special ed. classes, or about taking them out. They know nothing can be done as regards this problem without their signature. They know they can demand certain services if it is determined that their child needs such services, even though those services might not be offered in the school their child currently attends. The school district has to provide them somehow.

The LBD teacher has to be, then, something of a minor diplomat. Dealings with the parents must be so professional that only right and proper communications take place between the parents and teacher. Yet the teacher has also to demonstrate to the parent a certain love, tenderness, and caring for the child involved. The LBD teacher has to be a real person who experiences discouragement as well as delight in the student's performance. The LBD teacher has to care about the parents who care about the child.

Sometimes it may happen that a teacher does not like one of the kids in class. This happens to good teachers, to bad teachers, to regular program teachers, and to LBD teachers. It may be possible to transfer the child to another LBD teacher's room. If it is not possible to do this, it will require every ounce of human understanding to deal all year with that child and effectively help the child. Sometimes something magical happens somewhere along in the year, and the child responds to the teacher in a new and positive way, and the barriers are broken and they can like each other. This is one of the most creative, truly creative, experiences. It is a cause for rejoicing when it happens. Too often the teacher plods along feeling very guilty for not liking a student. How can a good teacher, one who has chosen a profession of helping the most needy of students in a system, not like a student? Simply because one is human, that's why. And because of being such a special human in the first place, one who even wanted this profession, at this low pay, with all these obstacles in the way, because of being so uniquely human, the LBD teacher will try, really try, to solve the problem of not liking a student.

What kind of training does one get for such a sensitive job? There are courses for special education in probably every education department of every college in the country. The public law has so brought special ed. into prominence that it is now quite popular to get a degree in one of the areas of special ed. It is certainly an area where there is an ever-increasing demand for teachers. And so the colleges are providing the courses and the needed degrees.

Scholarships may be available from local charitable organizations that have money specially earmarked for the benefit of handicapped children. Some school systems are so desperate for special ed. teachers that they are helping to finance the education of those teachers, at least at the graduate level. The U.S. Department of Education offers a grant for Handicapped Personnel Preparation, to provide assistance to those who are preparing to teach handicapped children. The address for information about this grant source is:

Dr. Jasper Harvey, Director, Division of Personnel Preparation
Office of Education
Bureau of Education for the Handicapped
Department of Education
Washington, DC 20202   Phone: (202) 245–9886.

The Grants Register, a resource book available in your public library, can also provide information about private foundation grants for students who are interested in working with the handicapped.

One needs a regular high school diploma to be admitted to the undergraduate level schools of education. And one needs to pass the college entrance exams. On the Scholastic Aptitude Tests taken in high school, although the math scores are not unimportant, it is important to do well on the verbal parts of the tests, the reading and writing parts.

At the undergraduate level, the prospective LBD teacher will take a variety of courses as well as those in the major field, the education field. The student will take many courses from the liberal arts program, with more psychology and educational courses emphasized. There will be courses in different learning theories, in approaches to teaching reading, and in abnormal psychology, among others. At the graduate level there will be more of the same, with additional seminars and practicums. There will be some actual tutoring done through the practicums and testing of children who have been referred for special ed. help. Probably the college will have a "learning lab" of its own where parents can bring their children, for a fee, for remedial help. The parents know that in this situation, although the work with their children is being done by students, there is constant supervision by "master" teachers, specialists with Ph.D. degrees. The undergraduate students will be assigned to schools for "practice teaching" during their senior year. Most of the graduate students will already be teaching.

One of the points made on the *MacNeil/Lehrer Report* in June, 1980, about practice teaching was that there is not enough of it for any teachers, not just for special ed. teachers. It was felt by some present in the discussion that much more of teacher training time ought to be spent in actual classroom experience in order to alleviate the problems of teacher burn-out. It was felt that if the education students were better prepared for what they had to face in the classrooms today, they might be better able to cope with it. And some private agencies have arisen with the objective of helping teachers face what is in store for them in the classroom. These offer workshops, seminars, discussion groups to help teachers sort out all the problems and perhaps come to grips with them better. The only problem that wasn't precisely dealt with at one such place, said the manager, was that of special ed. kids, especially special ed. kids in the regular program. They could not, he felt, deal with everything.

A colleague, an LBD teacher out of college for two years, tells me that nothing she learned in college prepared her for what she had to face in the actual classroom. In college she learned about the "textbook" learning disabled child, the "classic" LD case. She does not meet such "classic" cases in her room. Nothing prepared her for what she is doing. She is, she tells me, teaching the "rejects" of the system, those kids who, because they "can't stay in their seats or have big mouths," are put in LBD rooms.

Another LBD teacher says she shocked her family by telling her younger, idealistic brothers and sisters to "forget special education" for a major. "You think it's going to be all this beautiful work of helping kids who need you and want to be helped. Forget it. It's not anything at all what I was prepared for in my college classes for special education."

Another LBD teacher says, "Nothing they ever taught me has anything to do with what goes on in this school day in and day out."

After a long pause another LBD teacher responds, "I'm just trying to think if there was one class, maybe, that prepared me for school. I don't think so. No, I can't think of any."

And yet another LBD teacher says, "I learned by going and doing it. I learned how to teach by teaching. None of my college classes prepared me for teaching. None of them."

The representative from the National Council of Colleges said on the *MacNeil/Lehrer Report* that they are aware that colleges of education are not providing any teachers, not just special ed. teachers, with adequate skills to cope with today's classrooms. They are working on solutions. One of the solutions seems to be to provide more classroom experience for the school of education student.

The LBD teacher will be provided with continuing in-service programs. These programs are usually in the evening and are offered by the school system. A stipend may be offered for attendance at these, or they may be used in exchange for a free day for the teacher taking them on a day when other teachers would have to report for in-service at school.

National organizations, such as the ACLD, sponsor a convention every year. The Council for Exceptional Children (CEC) holds a yearly convention also. The speakers are usually good at these conventions, and they represent a broad spectrum of people interested in the field of special ed. Parents, professors, teachers, and all kinds of therapists are represented. These conventions can be sources of great inspiration and information for the beleaguered LBD teacher.

The special ed. teacher candidate has a lot to think about. Besides being sure of one's skills in reading, writing, and math, there are considerations to be made about one's attitudes about people. How well do you get along with others? Can you take part in group projects easily, play well on a team? How do you feel about authority figures, about the "establishment," about the "system"? How do you feel about members of other races? How do you feel about people who are "failures"? How do you see yourself? Failure? Well-rounded? Terrific kid? Shy? A problem? Nice? A loner? A loser?

Here is how Alice saw herself.

Chapter VII

Teaching the Learning-Behavior Disorder Class

BEN: *The teachers in here come out with straight answers and stuff. I mean they don't hesitate or nothing like that.*

What does an LBD teacher do?

The LBD teacher fills out forms, forms, and more forms. There are forms for the teacher and parents to fill out when the child is referred for testing, when the testing is completed and a conference on placement is held, and when the child receives the educational program for a year. There are forms to fill out to request the parents' presence at an annual review of the child's performance. There is a new educational program to write up each year.

Thus, the LBD teacher needs good verbal skills, needs to be able to write behavioral objectives, needs to be able to write fluent sentences, needs to be able to spell accurately. The LBD teacher needs a certain facility with words or the technical side of the job can be very draining. It may mean the difference between hours of after-school time spent making out individualized programs for children and something that can be accomplished in an easier time framework.

The LBD teacher takes part in hundreds of conferences on children. Every year there should be at least one conference on each child in the LBD program. There may be more than that. A parent, or a teacher, may request a conference at any time.

The LBD teacher needs to be able to take part in these conferences in such a way as to put the parents at ease in spite of the fact that

51

grave problems in their child's school life may be being discussed. The LBD teacher needs to be able to show the parents a sample of the child's work, an example of the materials used in that classroom, and an example of the kind of testing that is done in the LBD room. The LBD teacher should be able to tell the parents what the child is achieving in some of the mainstream programs. The LBD teacher should maintain such close contact with the child's other teachers that a general report can be furnished to the parents when those teachers cannot be present at a conference.

The LBD teacher assumes a unique responsibility for the children in the LBD room. The teacher must search out and determine *why* a child is not learning a certain concept. Then the LBD teacher must figure out *how* to help the child eventually to learn the concept. This may be done with a flow chart system by which the teacher is continually able to discern what is the next simplest concept in a sequence and thus plan an educational program for the child that relies on mastery of structural material before attacking new learning.

The LBD teacher needs always to be aware of new ideas for presenting material. It must be remembered that, in most cases, the LBD teacher is teaching material that the child has already heard a "hundred" times—and has failed at. If there is to be success this time around, there has to be an initially fresh approach to the subject matter. The LBD teacher needs to have available ready references for activities, games, challenging ways to put ideas across. The LBD teacher has to be something of a magician. This teacher seemingly has to produce something out of nothing, achievement where only failure existed.

Above all else, the LBD teacher needs to be a very honest person. Probably these children in the LBD class were assured by someone somewhere in their school histories that they were "doing just fine." And now look what has happened to them! It is very difficult for them to trust anyone in school again. It is very difficult for them to trust teachers. Sometimes with the older children it is helpful to show them their educational test scores, the scores that reflect what grade level they are performing on in reading or math. One must always keep in mind that the older the LBD kids are, the more they want to get out of that special classroom and get back with the "normal" kids. Sometimes it can be very helpful to explain to a child just where he or she is reading and what level needs to be achieved in order to return to the regular program. In that way the child may be drawn more easily into the process of planning his or her own program. The impetus is there then, and the teacher just needs to help keep it going by providing for successful learning activities in the striving for the goal.

These, then, are the things that you must keep in mind as you prepare to apply for a job as an LBD teacher. You will have no difficulty finding places to apply to for teaching jobs. The bulletin boards in the halls of the schools of education in colleges around the country are cluttered with requests for special ed. teachers. The Department of Education in your own locale would be a good place to start. Newspapers frequently print want ads for special ed. teachers from many other parts of the country. Professional magazines often list job opportunities for LBD and other special ed. teachers in many of the areas of the U.S. The publications of ACLD and CEC often list job opportunities all over the country for special ed. teachers.

Then you must prepare your résumé. The résumé should be typed. If you are not sure of the format for a good résumé, have a professional typist do this for you and have several copies made. Keep it in outline form and try to include anything that might have anything to do with the job you are applying for. For instance, if you worked at an Easter Seal summer camp as a counselor, this would be very useful on your résumé, as that job would have provided you with some firsthand experience with many handicapped children. A sample résumé might include:

Name
Address
Phone (with area code)

Career Goal: A brief statement of one or two sentences

Education: Undergraduate college
             Address
             Degree earned

             Graduate School
             Address
             Degree earned

             Extra credit courses taken at the college level

Experience: Summer camp for handicapped
             Growing up with a brother or sister who was in LBD
             Student teaching

Related Experience: Any workshop participation with parents of LBD children

Any private tutoring

Membership in organizations such as Big Brothers, Big Sisters

Certification: As an LBD teacher in what state for what grades

Honors and Awards: Scholastic

Athletic

Citizenship

Other Achievements: Participation in clubs, civic groups, etc.

Hobbies:

Personal: Birthdate

Age

Health

Marital status

Height

Weight

Hair

Eyes

Race

Sex

References: List three giving:

Name

Address

When the replies from your résumés come flowing in, the next task is to prepare for the interview. Dress professionally. No slacks or jeans for women. No tee shirts for men. Be well-groomed.

During the interview try not to appear nervous, tense. Ask questions. You are aware of what it means to take on the job for which you are applying, and feel confident enough of yourself to ask any questions that you may have. Find out about the financial benefits of the job. Ask about the kinds of insurance provided for teachers, the hospital and medical provisions of the system. Ask what type of pension fund the system has. Some school systems deduct Social Security contributions for their employees, but not all do this. Some school systems have their own retirement funds and do not make Social Security deductions. Most systems offer opportunities for tax-sheltered annuities from several companies. Get the names and addresses of these for future reference. Find out about the credit union that this system probably has for the benefit of employees. Through the credit union, loans to system employees are more easily obtainable than through banks and at times may be at a cheaper interest rate. Ask about sick leave. Ask about anything that you consider an important right for an employee to have. Ask about the rights of students.

But then, the preliminaries will be over and you will be hired. Because they really need you, you will be hired. Some systems are so desperate for special ed. teachers that they are hiring teachers with less than ten hours of graduate-level work toward a special ed. degree.

Then you can start worrying about IEP's, the Individualized Educational Programs that you must make out for each student. Then you can start worrying about parent conferences. Then you can start worrying about teaching that unique creature, the LBD child.

In planning an instructional program for a child, a whole range of knowledge is needed by the teacher. The LBD teacher, especially, needs to know how to break information down into its smallest components. It has been said that the best teachers in an entire system are the first-grade teachers. This is so because they, more than any others, know how to break information down so that it is readily understandable. The LBD teacher has to be able to do this very thing. The children in the LBD room have, by and large, failed to comprehend material sufficiently to achieve mastery because of the failure of someone, or a lot of someones, to do just this.

It is helpful to use a flow chart when planning to teach a particular concept. This is a great aid in conditioning the teacher to think in terms of breaking the material down so that it can be readily understood. If a child does not grasp the immediate concept being taught, the idea then is to determine what is the next simplest task in sequence and teach it. It may require going back several steps in sequence before the problem area, the bottom line, as it were, is found. It may be necessary to go from the abstract concepts being taught at a certain level to the most basic, concrete elements of a problem before it is understood. Thus, when a child cannot master the technique of, say, short division, of dividing a three-digit numeral by a two-digit numeral, the following steps might be taken in trying to locate where it is in the sequence that the child experiences initial difficulty:

SHORT DIVISION: THREE-DIGIT NUMERAL
DIVIDED BY TWO-DIGIT NUMERAL

$$(26\overline{)182})$$

| if;
| not
↓

Can the child "estimate" the 25's in 175? Can the child "see" the similarity with 26 into 182?

| if;
| not
↓

Can the child divide a two-digit number by one digit?

$$(6\overline{)84})$$

| if;
| not
↓

Can the child divide? Does the child use the "division tables" with facility?

| if;
| not
↓

Can the child multiply, use the "multiplication tables" with facility?

| if;
| not
↓

Can the child count in groups (by 5's, 7's, 4's, etc.)?

| if;
| not
↓

Can the child put numbers in an ordered sequence? (5,3,6,4,5,3,_,4)

| if;
| not
↓

Can the child count by one's?

| if;
| not
↓

Can the child put pictures in an ordered sequence? (story line pictures, for instance, or pictures of the seasons)

if not ↓

Can the child put manipulative tools in sequence? (blocks of: red, blue, yellow, green, red, blue, yellow, green)

if not ↓

Does the child know the colors?

if not ↓

Can the child build a train of objects by feeling the concreteness of *one plus* something else, *plus one* more, *plus one* more, etc.?

Every concept taught in the LBD room ought to be planned with the possibility that it may need to be broken down into its simplest, most concrete level of components. The challenge is to find at what point in this progression of knowledge it is that the child is "stuck." It is not usually necessary to reach all the way back to the most elemental forms of knowledge, but it is necessary to understand the developmental process of learning, how the mind progresses from the concrete to the abstract, in order to find the place where the child is lost.

An example of a flow chart that could be used in any instance is shown on page 58.

It is a recycling process that is continuous until remediation is complete. The teacher makes use of all the feedback information from tests, daily work, and oral responses to plan the program for each child. Teacher observation is one of the most valuable aids in obtaining this feedback. It is not always necessary to do formal testing to find out what one needs to know about a child's developmental stage of learning.

Once the teacher has this data, this information about a child, it is possible to write a behavioral objective for the child. So the child that was having difficulty with short division, for example, might have a behavioral objective written for him or her that includes a program of teaching and reinforcing some other skills needed for the mastery of the short division process. A behavioral objective has three parts:

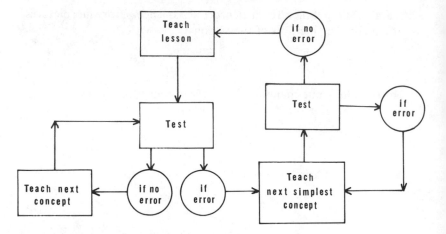

what is going to be taught, a time limit for teaching this, and the extent of mastery expected from the task.

If the child, Lydia, let's say, was "stuck" at the level of having difficulty with the multiplication tables, then an objective would be written for that skill to be mastered in a reasonable amount of time and with sufficient mastery that the next task could be achieved with less difficulty. Thus:

Given daily instruction in the multiplication tables for four weeks, Lydia will be able to recall the tables, both orally and in writing, with 90 percent accuracy. Then:

Given daily instruction in the division tables for two weeks, Lydia will be able to recall these, both orally and in writing, with 90 percent mastery. Then:

Given daily instruction in division of a two-digit number by a one-digit number for two weeks, Lydia will be able to perform this operation with 90 percent accuracy. Finally one can be written:

Given daily instruction in division of a three-digit number by a two-digit number for three weeks, Lydia will be able to perform this operation with 90 percent accuracy.

It is necessary to keep in mind here also that in accomplishing just one simple task, like teaching a child to understand the concept of "one plus," many modifications may be used and written into the objectives. Thus:

Given daily practice in bouncing a ball, Lydia will be able to count from "one plus one" to "five plus one" after one week with 100 percent accuracy. Or:

Given daily practice with a set of blocks (or Cuisenaire Rods), Lydia will be able to count from "one plus one" to "five plus one" after one week with 100 percent accuracy. Or:

Given daily practice with pencil and paper, Lydia will be able to draw sticks showing "one plus one" to "five plus one" after one week with 100 percent accuracy.

Many modifications can be brought into this task so that a lot of sensory experiences are provided for in the learning of "one plus—." There could be listening experiences provided, for instance listening to the teacher sing notes, or tap on the desk, or use a drum. There could be tasting experiences provided: orange segments, for instance, or peanuts.

Perhaps these could all be incorporated into one behavioral objective:

Given daily instruction for three weeks in the concept of "one plus—," by:
1. bouncing a ball and counting;
2. using the Cuisenaire Rods and counting;
3. marking a paper with sticks and counting;
4. listening to the teacher sing notes, tap a finger, beat a drum, while Lydia counts;
5. tasting orange segments and peanuts and counting;
Lydia will be able to count from "one plus one" to "one plus five" with 100 percent accuracy.

Now that all the information is in and you know where you are heading with a child, the Individualized Educational Program may be tackled. Here is a sample IEP:

INDIVIDUALIZED EDUCATIONAL PROGRAM

CHILD'S NAME   Lydia
ADDRESS   1387 Main St., New York, N.Y.
PRESENT SCHOOL ATTENDING   #39
CHILD'S I.D. NUMBER   23845
BIRTHDATE   7/11/7–
DATE OF ENTRANCE TO PROGRAM   5/1/8–

A. PRESENT LEVEL OF EDUCATIONAL PERFORMANCE
STRENGTHS:
Lydia reads well on grade level. She has good decoding skills. She follows written directions well. She does well in reading comprehension, scoring at grade level on achievement tests.

WEAKNESSES:
Lydia cannot divide a three-digit number by a two-digit number in arithmetic. She does not know the tables for either multiplication or division. She does not understand the concept of "estimating" for an answer in short division.

B. PRESENT LEVEL OF BEHAVIORAL PERFORMANCE
STRENGTHS:
Lydia is always on task in the LBD room. She stays in her seat until her work is completed. She takes part in all the activities of the class. She is friendly and well liked.

WEAKNESSES:
Lydia cannot stay on task in the mainstream class she is in. She moves around a lot in her seat. She cries when corrected. She fights with other children.

C. COMMITTEE RECOMMENDATIONS, PLACEMENT AND COMMENTS
Lydia should remain in LBD for a longer period of time each day until she can handle more time in the regular program. She will now stay in LBD for three out of six hours of the school day.

D. EXTENT OF PARTICIPATION IN REGULAR EDUCATION PROGRAM
50%

E. DATE OF NEXT REVIEW
midterm grading period

F. ANNUAL GOALS BASED ON CHILD'S PRESENT LEVEL OF PERFORMANCE
Given daily instruction in math, Lydia will be able to divide a three-digit number by a two-digit number with 90% accuracy.

G. SHORT-TERM INSTRUCTION OBJECTIVE FOR EACH ANNUAL GOAL (Including objective criteria for evaluations of each objective)
Given daily instruction in the multiplication tables for four weeks, Lydia will be able to recall these, in writing and orally, at 90% accuracy.

Given daily instruction in the division tables for two weeks, Lydia will be able to recall these, both orally and in writing, with 90% accuracy.

Given daily instruction in "estimating" answers, Lydia will be able to estimate short division answers with 90% accuracy after three weeks. Use will be made of:

1. Cuisenaire Rods
2. money
3. flannel-board materials

Given daily instruction in short division for two months, Lydia will be able to divide three-digit numbers by two-digit numbers with 90% accuracy. TEACHER OBSERVATIONS, TEACHER-MADE TESTS, AND STANDARDIZED TESTS WILL BE USED.

H. SCHEDULES FOR REVIEW, EVALUATIONS OF OBJECTIVES
A review will occur at each grading period. For the year 198–, these are: Jan. 26; June 14.

I. SPECIAL EDUCATION AND RELATED SERVICES
Placement in the LBD room for 50% of the school day.

J. PROJECTED DATES FOR INITIATION AND ANTICIPATED DU-RATION OF SERVICES
5/1/8– through 6/24/8–.

According to the Federal guidelines, the IEP is to be filled out in the presence of the parents at the yearly conference. That is very difficult to accomplish, for a variety of reasons:

1. It will be impossible to produce a nice typed program given the circumstances of a conference.
2. Several teachers will need to have input on specific behavioral objectives. Teachers who instruct the child for different subjects ought to have equal chance to give observations, to plan programs for the child. In some instances this difficulty is dealt with by "homogenizing" the observations and making a general plan for the child that is fairly acceptable to all. This is not fair to the child, however. It does not allow for the very basic fact that a child may perform much better for one teacher than for another, in one subject area than another. Thus, the math teacher may have quite negative things to report about a child's behavior and performance in that class, whereas the reading teacher may see a different child entirely. Each teacher ought to have the chance to comment on the attitude and performance of the child if a total picture of that child is to emerge. It should not be left to one teacher to write up the observations when more than one teacher is involved in the educational process. The child may emerge from one person's description as a very difficult child or as one who is entirely cooperative, depending on the bias of the

teacher writing the report. It is in the child's best interest that a full, well-rounded picture be developed of him or her, even though this may result in an IEP that is not "picture perfect." The IEP's are for the benefit of the children and the parents, however, and not for the edification of whatever administrative personnel finally receive a copy at the central office.

3. Parents must agree to all that is written and planned for the child. The parents must sign the IEP as a stamp of approval on the educational program being outlined for the child. Thus it may happen that they would prefer an item, or items, to be altered in the program. If the LBD teacher has come to the conference with the program all written out in advance, it will be impossible to make the necessary changes and to protect the rights of all parties concerned. If parents do not attend any scheduled conferences during the year, they seem to forfeit their right in this area, and the teacher plans the program independently, sending the papers home for signatures upon their completion.

4. The LBD teacher needs to come to the conference very well prepared and able to discuss all the observations and behavioral objectives with accuracy and ease. The teacher must come to the conference prepared to be very specific.

Not much has been mentioned here about the programs for helping the more behaviorally disordered students to become "rehabilitated." Usually a process of behavior modification of some sort is employed by the LBD teacher to help the child improve behavior, or be "cured," as the saying goes. In such a program of behavior modification, the teacher determines what rewards will be effective for an individual child, effective enough that the child will eventually stop the unsatisfactory behavior altogether. "Rewards" have come to have a bad association for some people. Teachers are not really trying to "buy" children by rewarding them for improving their behavior. They are simply giving them attention for doing something positive for a change. These children have learned that negative behavior has brought a lot of attention, of one kind or another, and now some attention for being "good" is in order if they are to be "weaned" from misconduct. The rewards are not always candy or material things either, although that is a popular misconception. It is necessary for the perceptive LBD teacher to find out what things might be rewarding to a child. This can result in some surprising information being revealed. A child may work very hard for some extra free time, or to be allowed time to draw, or to have a free homework night. Some teachers dispense "tokens" to their students for good behavior. These tokens may be used to "purchase" goods in the classroom: an extra trip to the drinking fountain; game-playing time; a rest period.

A behavioral objective might be:

Given a token for each successful effort, Ben will perform all tasks to completion for one week with 90 percent self-mastery.

That may be a hard goal to achieve. Goals cannot be so rigid, so impossible that the child becomes discouraged. Although the teacher surely hopes for 100 percent mastery over some behavior problems, it may be more realistic sometimes to plan for 80 percent improvement or 85 percent. The important thing in working with LBD children is to provide sufficient room for success for them. It is self-defeating, in any event, to be so idealistic that unreasonable goals are set for the children and for the teacher. These are, after all, children who have already experienced much failure and frustration, and the LBD teacher definitely does not want to become part of that all too familiar pattern for them.

This all seems like an incredible task, all these objectives and conferences and ideas for teaching strategies. Where does one ever learn them all?

There are plenty of resources for the LBD teacher. Talk to other teachers. Go to in-service workshops put on by the local school system. Subscribe to some of the national teacher magazines such as *Learning, The Grade Teacher, The Instructor.*

A marvelous publication is put out by a group called Good Apple, Inc., in Carthage, Illinois. Several times a year thay publish a "newspaper" composed entirely of ideas and teaching strategies sent in by teachers throughout the country. Teachers are paid a substantial sum for ideas published. A teacher may send in an idea for a full-page spread and receive $100, or for a half-page spread at $50. The ideas are always well illustrated and are accompanied by thorough instructions. It is an innovative and excellent example of sharing among teachers.

Special ed. has become "big business." There are publications and games and ditto books and manuals of all kinds just for special ed.

teachers. There are aids for the teacher of the hyperactive child, or the child with a short attention span, or the distractable student.

Two or three times a week I find in my home or school mailbox literature from various companies promoting special ed. materials. One is headed "Special Education Materials." It offers booklets, posters, study cards, filmstrips, audio cassettes, games, picture sets, sport, leisure, and recreation skills materials, physical education materials, daily living skills programs, learning activities, books, health education materials, and materials for mainstream teachers of special ed. kids.

In a monthly education publication six of the full-page ads are for special ed. materials.

Another special ed. catalog comes in. It advertises thus: "To us— all education is special." It offers: cognitive development workbooks, visual acuity screening charts, perceptual enhancement workbooks, figure-ground transparencies, visual closure cards, auditory perception programs, auditory discrimination programs, tactile learning cards, sensory-motor writing programs, motor coordination chalkboards, therapy kits. The catalog is 38 pages long.

There is a lot of money involved in special ed. materials. But a teacher need never feel so desperate for help, for new ideas, that no resources are available. For a price any teacher can find ideas and help from the marketplace. There is an answer available for every type of special ed. problem.

All of this is part of the "straight answers and stuff" that the special ed. kids feel is so important to their lives in this program. They know where they stand, what their problems are, how they are involved in the solution, and precisely what the program is that is being implemented in their remediation. This is the benefit, the bonus, that comes from all those hours of paperwork, of conferences, of planning IEP's, of searching for the right activities for the right child. Both the child and the teacher know exactly what is going on to help the child. It is a very straightforward, honest approach. It is very individualized, and for many children this is a novelty in their educational lives.

This approach helps them to think more clearly about themselves. Here is Kim's definition of herself.

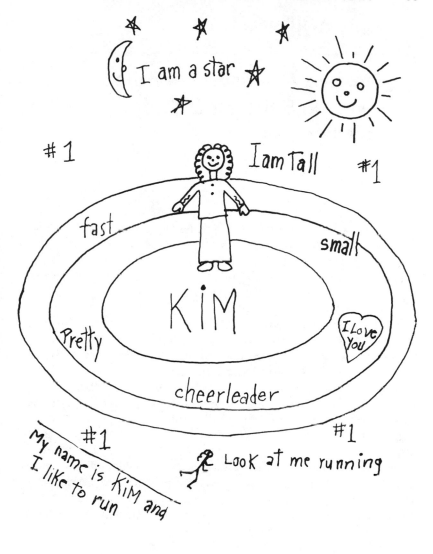

Chapter VIII

Creative Alternatives for the Learning-Behavior Disorder Teacher

KIT: *Like if you like the class you're in, you still have to leave and come up here, and do the same stuff till you're out on your level.*

BEN: *It would be nice if you could come up here just when you want to or feel you need to.*

So far we've talked about the "organization" person as the special ed. teacher. It must seem as if the only options open for people in the area of special ed. are as parts of systems where they must tread cautiously and speak softly for fear of upsetting someone's apple cart. This is the case in most public school systems. Remember, these are the systems that, because of policies and philosophies of rigidity, have very probably caused some of the LBD problems the special ed. teacher must now remediate. It seems sometimes as if it is all part of a self-perpetuating system. One way to keep the public schools operating is to get Federal money for the handicapped. The public schools by their very policies turn out more clients in need of special ed. services every year. The system feeds, as it were, on its very failures. The schools are helped to remain open by the Federal money to remediate the kids who failed in the schools.

But the picture does not have to be all that bleak for a teacher. There are some other, more creative options for the special ed. teacher. The area of special ed. offers some possibilities other than a lifetime of service to the classrooms of the public schools.

It was mentioned earlier that the burn-out rate for special ed. teachers is about three years. Many special ed. teachers plan ahead so that, by that time in their careers, they will be able to make a move up the ladder in the system. There are jobs for these former special ed. teachers as consultants, instructional coordinators, members of testing teams, or as supervisors if courses in supervision are taken. If that is the direction a teacher is headed in, some careful preparation needs to be done, as the competition for these jobs is keen. Remember that there are many other burned-out teachers, or simply other teachers who have ambitions to move up and out of the classrooms, who are seeking the same jobs as you. The public schools are equal opportunity employers, so they have to advertise jobs widely enough that interested parties are made aware of them. Most systems have a bulletin that is published from the central office and sent out to all employees. This is one way that job openings are advertised. Systems have a certain phone line that, when dialed, gives a recording of all the current positions available. A time limit is stated in which to send in applications for the job, and all the necessary qualifications are given.

Then it is time to update the résumé, and there should be many more activities to list. By this time you should belong to several professional organizations. If you really want to move up in the system, it is advisable to make yourself very visible before you make that move. It is not enough just to be a good teacher and a nice person. One needs to take part in many of the outside activities of the department. Attend extra workshops, volunteer to teach some of the workshops. Work on special projects with your class and be sure to invite the principal, the supervisor, the parents. Have some special parent workshops in the evenings. Take extra courses in your field, so that you keep abreast of new information, new ideas. Be visible. That is a very important point. Make sure that your successes are noticed. Tell people when you do a good job. Be recognized for your achievements. Then list those achievements in your résumé. It won't be long before you have an impressive résumé.

Be sure to keep a constantly growing file of good reference letters. You may have a folder in the Alumnae Association of your college. You will have a folder on file at the central office of your school system. Ask every principal, every supervisor, every team leader you work with to write a letter of recommendation for that folder. Get letters from people you work with, from parents of children whom you teach.

And then, again, because these systems are equal opportunity employers, there will be another interview. Be positive. If you are seeking advancement in a system that rewards the team player, then be that. If this is your choice, your goal, advancement in this system, then it makes sense to appear to appreciate the system. Again, ask questions. Ask about salary and hours and benefits and responsibilities. There will probably be several persons interviewing you in this session, and each will have definite questions to put to you. It is a bit more strenuous than the more informal interview of initial hiring. Again, there are probably many people competing for this same job, so the interviewing process is more critical.

Or after three years, if you are burned out, or maybe just because it appeals to you, you might want to teach in a college program. You might want to teach teachers of special ed. kids. Usually you need a doctorate in the field of special education to do this. Here are some advertisements taken from the magazine *Exceptional Children:*[9]

ASSISTANT/ASSOCIATE PROFESSORS OF SPECIAL EDUCA-TION. Full-time (1) and part-time (3) faculty to work with graduate programs in Special Education. Responsibilities include graduate level teaching, supervising, and advising. Annual contract with the possibility that the full-time position will be converted to a tenure-track appointment. Qualifications include: earned doctorate in special education or related fields; 2 years teaching experience with handicapped children; strong background in diagnostic teaching; and demonstrated research and scholarly ability.

THE SCHOOL OF EDUCATION anticipates two tenure-accruing positions in Special Education: Associate/Full Professor–earned doctorate, substantial research/publication record, minimum 3 years experience as teacher/supervisor—early childhood handicapped. To teach/advise masters and doctoral level students, participate in admin. of pre-K handicapped program, coordinate/conduct programmatic research. Salary—competitive. Assistant Professor–earned doctorate, evidence of teaching excellence and research/publication potential, minimum 3 years experience as teacher/supervisor–severely handicapped. To teach/advise masters and doctoral level, conduct programmatic research. Salary—competitive. EOE

SPECIAL EDUCATION: ASSISTANT PROFESSOR (tenure track) or visiting assistant professor to teach courses in mental retardation (mild to profound), supervise practica in mental retardation and supervise student teachers. Doctorate in special education required with emphasis in MR and developmental disabilities. Classroom experience with exceptional persons required.

Or if you prefer to start out entirely differently in your career as a special ed. teacher, try one of the private schools that operate solely for the purpose of remediating special ed. kids. There are private schools of this type in nearly every community of the country, as more and more parents become frustrated with public education. Indeed, one such school in South Carolina goes so far as to encourage a certain amount of "chaos" in the school, so that the students will be better able to adapt to public schools when they return. Here is an advertisement for another private special ed. school:

THE VANGUARD SCHOOL[10]

LAKE WALES, FLORIDA
Harry E. Nelson, M.Ed., President

The Vanguard School is a coed boarding and day school designed for young people 6–18, grades 1–12, who present a varying spectrum of learning related disorders. The 75-acre campus, three miles north of the city of Lake Wales, contains 2 residence halls, school building, dining hall, multipurpose recreational and workshop building and the Edward Bartsch Memorial Gym.

The academically oriented program provides educational opportunities which allow for skill acquisition along developmental lines, and strives to prepare students for transition to a regular school or to the next stage toward self-sufficiency. Each major area of the student's development—including intellectual, social, emotional, physical and moral—is integrated into the learning and living experience. Remedial in nature, the curriculum is highly individualized since each student presents a unique constellation of strengths and weaknesses which must be considered in planning the student's total program. The learning disabled child profits from the healthy competiveness of a small homogeneous class. Classrooms are equipped with advanced educational aids to inculcate essential skills, understandings and insights. Learning activities are explicit, steps gradual and uniform, class structure carefully controlled.

Children with disturbances in communication receive individual program emphasis in language development, speech therapy and auditory training. Those with inadequate perceptual function have special visual-motor training. Others, whose neuromuscular coordination is atypical, are aided with motor activities and perceptual competence training. Individual remedial reading and math are provided for students who can benefit from specific help. For the older student, a program of career and vocational orientation stresses practical learning and the development of prerequisites for successful employment in the future.

Water sports, swimming, boating, fishing, tennis and basketball are but a few of the athletic features. Faculty and staff believe study, physical education and recreation equip students to successfully deal with the demands of social interaction.

Admission policies are non-discriminatory in terms of race, color, creed, ethnic or national origin. Additional day schools are located in Paoli, Pennsylvania, and Coconut Grove, Florida. Write or call (813) 676–6091.

There are opportunities in the private school sector. Start your own school for LBD kids. Federal grants are available to nonprofit groups in the area of special education. Information about possible funding sources can be obtained through ERIC, or The ERIC Clearinghouse on Handicapped and Gifted Children. This is a resource of The Council for Exceptional Children. The address is:

The Council for Exceptional Children
1920 Association Drive
Reston, VA 22091   (703) 620–3660

A recent ERIC notice contained information about:[11]

1. Directory for Exceptional Children
2. Directory for Special Children
3. Directory of Educational Facilities for the Learning Disabled
4. Yearbook of Special Education

Invaluable information about possible funding sources can be obtained from ERIC. This is just another reason why CEC membership is so important for the special ed. teacher. The CEC is one of the most vital sources of information about everything that touches the lives of special ed. children. An ERIC search provided one teacher with access to the following book:

Handicapped Funding Directory[12]
By Burton J. Eckstein
from
Research Grant Guides
P.O. Box 357
Oceanside, NY 11572

This publication costs $16.50 and contains every possible funding source for someone who wants to go into the business of a special school, or even other special ed. projects. One such grant available for LD kids is Special Programs for Children With Specific Learning Disabilities. The guide lists all the pertinent information the potential applicant needs to know about this grant:

1. Federal agency—U.S. Department of Education
2. Authorization—Education for Handicapped Children Act
3. Objectives—To establish and operate model centers for the improvement of education of children with specific learning disabilities, through research and training of personnel
4. Types of assistance—project grants

It goes on to list eligibility requirements, application procedures, and funds available for grant awards. This particular grant award is for innovative and creative projects that can be replicated throughout the country.

The *Handicapped Funding Directory* provides hints on how to write grant proposals. It outlines the factors the examiners look for in appraising a grant application. It gives state-by-state funding sources for programs for the handicapped.

One is not locked into the barren stretches of public education. There are alternatives. Another possibility is to become a teacher of the learning disabled at the junior college or college level. More and more students are leaving high school with their learning problems intact and unremediated. Remember that these students have average or above average IQ's and deserve the chance to go to college. Sometimes all they need is the systematic approach and breakdown of information that a seasoned LBD teacher can provide. It is difficult for the college faculty, who have never had to do so, to break down their lectures into the most easily understandable components. An LBD teacher is trained to do just that.

One college dean, who herself has a Ph.D. in Special Education, says that more and more of these students are coming out of the public schools every year and heading for the small, private college campuses, because, she says, "They say they know we will take care of them here, whereas on the state university campuses they will get lost in the crowd." There is ample room on these campuses for LBD teachers to provide developmental math, reading, and writing skills, she feels.

Much exciting research is being done about the brain. Someone has said that the frontier for the last few years of the twentieth century will be that of brain research. More and more is being written about the hemispheres of the brain, particularly the right hemisphere. This is the area that controls creative thought, intuitive thinking. The left hemisphere controls verbal skills, reading, language, reasoning.

Our children in LBD have usually failed so miserably at verbal activities that one wonders what are the possibilities for approaching remediation with an emphasis on right-hemisphere skills. Even epileptics have been taught some language usage through the use of their right hemispheres when the bridge between the hemispheres, the corpus callosum, was severed to reduce seizures.

There are exciting possibilities with the use of computers for specific remedial programs. Many computer terminals are accompanied by software in remedial math and reading skills. The PLATO IV advertises, for instance, that after twenty-five hours of use students can improve one year to one and one-half years in reading and as much as two years in math. This is the equivalent of twenty-five days of class time for one hour per day. If such progress can truly be made, the possibility exists to help a child make 400 or even 500 percent gains in a year. Texas Instruments advertises remedial programs in software, as do APPLE TWO and APPLE THREE. Computers also provide many creative thinking exercises.

Children particularly love to do their math work on calculators such as the Classmate Eighty-Eight put out by The Monroe Co. They can even challenge each other to races on a certain series, the winner being the child who gets the most correct in the shortest time.

Why aren't there more special schools for special kids with all these exciting, innovative techniques in use? Milton Friedman has suggested the use of vouchers for money given by the Federal government to parents for the education of their children. The government spends about $2,000 per child in the regular programs throughout the country. An average of about $3,000 is spent on the special ed. children. In his book and on the television program, both called *Free to Choose,* Friedman outlined the advantages of a voucher system of education. Each child's parents would receive a certain sum of money from the government to spend according to personal choice for the child's education. If the parents wanted to put their child in a small private school that offered specific remedial programs, they would have the wherewithal to do just that. In this kind of setup all children, those from disadvantaged as well as from economically advantaged homes, would have the opportunity for small schools and private education. It just needs to capture the public's imagination. It is an idea that needs to catch on. There might be a proliferation of schools, such as The Vanguard School of Florida, if this kind of public financing were available for all to take advantage of.

There might even, eventually, be an end to the need for remedial services to the extent that they are now provided, if different kinds of educational opportunities were open to all children for all of their school lives.

Children certainly would not have to be "pull-out" children or "part-timers" anymore. They wouldn't have to leave regular programs, because they would be part of a regular program in a special school.

This is an example in *syncretism.* The children brainstormed some ideas about school. First they thought of some common nouns. These were the words brainstormed by Ben and Alice and Kit and Adam and Lydia and Chuck.

trucks	hippo	bread	park
dogs	thermometer	chairs	ice cream
butter	cats	swimming pool	cheese

They chose *cheese* for the exercise. We used the sentence then: *School Is Like Cheese.*

Then they closed their eyes and "felt" that they were cheese. When they opened their eyes, these were the words they used to describe cheese.

smelly	stale	holey	brick	circle
yellow	moldy	rotten	hard	rubbery
soft	spreads	melty	triangle	

Next the children matched up the words so that the two words that formed a pair were not exactly alike nor exactly opposite. This is how they matched them.

smelly-melty	rotten-brick
circle-yellow	rubbery-triangle
soft-holey	hard-moldy
spreads-stale	

Then we made the comparisons. They agreed with the pairings as truly fitting their images of school in nearly every instance.

1. Is school smelly and melty? YES
2. Is school a circle and yellow? SOMETIMES
3. Is school soft and holey? YES
4. Is school stale and does it spread? YES
5. Is school rotten and brick? YES
6. Is school rubbery and a triangle? SOMETIMES
7. Is school hard and moldy? YES

Chapter IX

The School That Hummed

BEN: *I wish I could get out of LD. Right now. Right today.*
CHUCK: *I'd leave this very minute, if I could.*

It is possible, even in a public school, for the attitudes toward special ed., as well as toward everything else about learning in that school, to be positive. A school like that could be said to have a special kind of harmony about it. It hums.

There was a school that hummed. Anywhere you went in this school you could hear the hum: the hall, the lunchroom, the classrooms, the teachers' lounge. There was always the sound of a lovely, melodic, soft hum in every corner of the building. It was a happy, lyrical, lilting sound that sort of captured everyone's ear, made everyone sing along, or hum along. The kids and teachers and the principal could be caught at any time going about their work of reading, or teaching, or running the school while they were humming.

The school won the notice of people all over the country because it hummed. Educators and reporters came from all over the country to examine and report on this school. The school got national recognition. It received many grants for its special programs because in every activity that occurred there a lot of good things were accomplished and people enjoyed working together. They hummed.

It became a real community school. The parents and other community people were very much involved in this school. The parents had a great say in all the policies of the school. In a sense they "owned" the school. They determined the courses they wanted taught. The parents could even decide on what teachers were going to teach in the school.

75

The school was open after hours for community people who wanted to use it. Some of the teachers and some of the community people taught classes there in the evenings. Almost any time of the day or night you could drop by and find this school "open."

The teachers were excited about their students and about teaching them. They tried all sorts of methods to help the kids improve in reading, math, and writing. They tried many innovative techniques to interest

3. A Humming day at the Humming School

the students in the world around them, in science, in geography and history. The kids loved school. A lot of real learning went on. There wasn't always 100 percent success with everything, but the children were happy. They loved coming to a school that had such a peaceful, joyous hum. They didn't want to miss a day if they could help it.

The mornings were especially filled with excitement. There was always the anticipation of what new project, new idea, the teachers would involve them in that day. Often there were special projects, big projects, like painting murals for the walls of the front hall. For this, they painted scenes from their neighborhood. They managed to capture some idea of the history of the neighborhood in some of the scenes. They caught a pride in the neighborhood throughout the whole mural.

There were always workshops going on in this school. The staff and the parents put them on together. The staff and the parents worked well together. They seemed to respect each other, even like each other. Everyone always seemed to have something to say and wanted to share it with others. A lot of overtime was put in by staff. A lot of extra time away from home was put in by parents. No one was ever paid for all the extra time service. They worked on things that could benefit the whole community. They operated a small repair shop in the school, had nutrition workshops, and had a library for the adults of the neighborhood. They taught some first-aid classes in the school. Sewing lessons were offered, and adult level reading and math classes. There was a small museum on the top floor, filled with things that represented the history of the neighborhood.

But the children always came first. Teachers were always planning ways to please the children. They made their rooms especially bright and attractive. They took the students on wonderful field trips after school hours. They went camping with them for a week at a time every spring and fall. These trips were during school time. Back at school there was a little park in the next block where teachers and children often went for a game of soft-ball during recess.

Mr. Carster was the principal of this school, but he didn't act like a boss. He allowed people to make up their own minds about things. He never got upset about the crazy things kids do. He liked kids.

Children felt at home in this school. It may have been the hum that made them so relaxed, so happy. They weren't always trying to get away with things the way kids usually do in most schools. They just sort of acted normal here and enjoyed school life.

Once everyone was looking all over the place for Brent. Someone had seen him come in before the starting bell sounded, but now he seemed to be missing. In a little while, Brent appeared at his classroom door and got ready to go to work. Where had he been? It was the first snowfall of the year, and Brent had been irresistibly drawn to the playground. He just wanted to feel the first snow on his face, taste it, catch it in his hair. Then he was satisfied to come in and to go to work. He hummed all day.

The special ed. classes were especially appealing to youngsters in this school. Children actually came up to the LBD teachers and asked when it would be their turn to come into these classes. Everyone in the school had a positive attitude about special ed. The mainstream staff showed their respect for the LBD classes and for the teachers who taught them. They helped the children realize what a wonderful chance they were getting to improve their skills by going to LBD. The kids who didn't get to come to the special ed. rooms were often very disappointed, so the regular teachers often invited the LBD teachers to come to their classes and teach some classes with them. In that way all the children could feel they were getting that extra special help that the kids got who went to special ed.

With such a marvelous school in operation, with everyone all over the country admiring it and coming to get ideas for schools back home, you just know that this school was considered pretty special in its own school district, don't you? Surely the superintendents and the school board were proud of this school? And surely they tried to make other schools that hummed so well in the rest of the district?

No. Just the opposite, in fact.

The central office people, the superintendents, and the board tried their best to stifle that hum, to choke it, to silence it. They tried to repaint the walls, to cover the children's mural with a sort of gray-green paint. They tried to close the school. They tried very hard to close the school. They had special meetings just to plan strategies for closing this school.

Many, many parents and teachers and community people got up at this meeting to tell what the school meant to them. None of them had ever gone to a school that hummed, and now that they had one for these children, they were not going to give it up. Mr. Carster told the board that, even though they paid him his salary, he felt he was an employee of the people whom he served in that community. He would operate the kind of school that they wanted for their children.

Well, the school stayed open and things continued to hum right along. But the rest of the school system hated that school, hated its hum. Teachers in other schools spread rumors about how dreadful things were in the humming school, that kids couldn't read, that it was wild there. They said the teachers didn't dress professionally. They said the parents had too much say there. The rumors got louder and louder, but never loud enough to drown out the hum at the community school. Almost, but not quite.

Then Mr. Carster retired. And, for a few years, different principals were sent there every year. The school continued to hum, but the tune faltered a little every now and then. The new principals exerted their own influence on the school. They threw their own weight around a lot more than Mr. Carster had ever done. All decisions were made by the principals. The people still had their meetings with the teachers. There were still workshops. There were still camping trips, and the kids still used the little park down the street. The hum hung around.

National experts still paid attention to the school. And grants still kept coming in for so many of the different programs at the place. People from all over the country came for one particular meeting and talked lovingly about that school.

"Why is it," asked one expert, "with people all over the country admiring the work you do at your school, that it isn't more popular in your own community? How come the residents of the whole community don't hear your hum?"

The principal replied, "Well, so many of the people in the neighborhood of this school are poor. They might have a button off a shirt or a tooth missing, and how would that look if their pictures got in the papers?"

That time the hum missed a few beats.

Then one of the LBD teachers got into it with the principal about the LBD kids. Faye had worked out a deal with the regular program teachers to take the LBD kids back into their own rooms for certain portions of the day. They would go in for certain classes of special interest or for those subjects the teachers thought they could handle. These teachers loved the children and thought it was good for them to be in the regular program as much as possible. Besides, how else is a behavior disordered child going to learn how to behave in a regular classroom if he or she hardly ever gets to attend classes in the regular program?

Someone even recalled that Mr. Carster had said once, "If I ground my son for denting the fender of the car and tell him that he can't drive the car again until I can trust him, what kind of sense would that make? How will I ever know if I can trust him?"

These regular program teachers were all exceptional human beings and very special teachers. It is difficult to find teachers who want to be bothered with the LBD kids. Usually, they figure that if the kids are supposed to be in special ed., that is where they ought to stay and they are the LBD teacher's problems. But, of course, this school hummed and maybe the teachers' attitudes about all kids helped to keep it humming. The teachers were special because they thought all the kids were special.

But when Faye started to implement this schedule of returning LBD kids to class during the day, the principal said, "NO." The LBD kids had to stay in the LBD room all day, every day, until they were "cured." Then they would be removed from the LBD program totally and fully mainstreamed. They would not, at that time, be LBD kids anymore. The principal told Faye she was doing such a terrific job and was such a terrific teacher that it would be a shame to move any kids out of her program for even a part of the day. They could leave her only when they were fully "cured."

Brent was in LBD, and his father didn't want him in the special ed. class all day long. So this principal gave him the choice of having Brent in LBD all day or in the regular program all day. Well, Brent's father knew Brent couldn't yet handle the regular program full time. Brent still had a way to go in catching up with the other kids. And he still tired easily and got distracted. So he agreed to put Brent in LBD, with Faye, full time. But he didn't like it. He simply felt helpless to do anything about it.

Faye went to the leaders of the parents' community board about this problem. The principal was there too, and told the parents that the LBD program in their school was terrible and something had to be done about it. The parents were confused. They were also afraid of this principal. And they couldn't even hear the hum from their school anymore, it was getting so faint.

A child advocate came to represent the LBD children at a special meeting. The advocate felt that each child's case ought to be taken individually. This might mean that some children would stay in LBD part time and go to regular classes part time as they had been doing. The advocate felt you had to look at what was best for the individual child and not just make blanket rules for all of the kids.

But she couldn't convince the principal, and she left in tears. She told the principal when she was leaving, "This is the only school I've ever seen where the teachers actually *want* the special ed. kids in their regular programs, and you're going to destroy that?"

The teachers fought with the principal about it in faculty meetings. "We feel," they said, "it is healthier for the LBD children to be with us for part of each day." But the principal refused to listen and even got members of the supervisory staff at the central office to come down and back up the decision that the LBD children should remain full time in that program until they were "cured." And so it was done.

It was never determined if the principal had ever heard the hum. But after this episode, there was no longer any hum in the school.

Brent is terribly unhappy in school now. So are all the other kids. Five teachers planned on transferring out of the school that year.

The principal told some reporters that there was no reason this school shouldn't be just like every other school in the system. The goal of this principal was to do just that, to make this into an ordinary school. One that didn't hum.

A sign was put up on the office bulletin board stating that no one may take children to the park in the next block unless the teacher signs up for it to be one of the two allowed field trips for the year. It will be conducted as a field trip with parental permissions and extra chaperones required.

At the end of the year, the board announced the final closing of this school. The hum would never be back.

The Man in Our Town[13]

There was a man in our town,
And he was wondrous wise,
He jumped into a bramble bush,
And scratched out both his eyes.

But when he saw his eyes were out,
With all his might and main,
He jumped into another bush,
And scratched them in again.

Chapter X

The Learning-Disabled Adult and Teaching Opportunities for the Learning Disabilities Teacher

ADAM: *I've been in LD all my life.*

Someone has said, "If God had known what schools would be like, He would have made kids different."

What happens to the LBD population after the school years are over? Where do "old" LBD students go? What does all this mean for LBD teachers?

Many LBD kids graduate from high school. Some may actually be fully remediated. More often than not, they are not remediated to the performance levels needed for them to make satisfactory career choices.

Many LBD kids never make it to graduation. A lot of them drop out when they are sixteen years old or soon thereafter.

Some LBD kids manage to get themselves suspended and finally expelled from school. The suspension rates are high for students with poor academic skills.

There are opportunities for those kids who never graduated to get their GED's later from adult education centers. The GED is the Graduate Equivalency Diploma. Armed with this, they will be able to apply for jobs that would have been closed to them before. It is absolutely essential to secure the GED in order to get the jobs that will make life better.

The adult education centers usually provide heavy doses of the same kinds of programs that were used on students their entire school lives. The same kinds of programmed readers, the same programmed math texts are in these centers that line the shelves of hundreds of school warehouses throughout the country. Why do they seem to work here when they proved inadequate to the task of remediation for given students years before? The difference now seems to be in the students. This is the last chance for most of them, and they know it. There is present now a motivation born of desperateness that never existed while the students were attending regular schools. They are simply determined to accomplish now what they couldn't manage to do earlier.

It happens, though, that even now some of these students cannot handle learning to read. In spite of increased motivation and the availability of help, there are still some who cannot accomplish what they set out to do, develop the reading or math skills needed to get their GED's and, eventually, jobs.

Very probably these individuals belong to the increasing numbers of people who are LD adults. These adults face failure in many areas of adult living. They often cannot get the jobs they want. They cannot function in a society that depends so much on reading in everyday life. Everywhere in their world they are accompanied by the sense of defeat, frustration, at their inability to perform this task that for most other seems so commonplace.

They are at the mercy of those in the marketplace who can read. They are particularly vulnerable to unscrupulous people who can cheat them out of profits, who can cheat them in business deals. They may have no way of knowing what a contract states. They may not be able to read the advertisements for products, nor the fine print in contracts.

A man whose car had been damaged in a minor accident kept returning to the home of the person who had hit his car. He had received from her all the information about her insurance company, and she assured him repeatedly that she had also informed them of her fault in the incident. Finally, after three days of requesting her to handle the whole thing with the insurance company, he admitted to her that he couldn't read, couldn't handle the claim himself.

There are many persons in prison who have never learned to read or write, who have felt victimized by a system all their lives, and who finally asserted themslves in methods of violence. People who have known mostly failure all their lives are particularly susceptible to becoming very defensive and thus potentially dangerous. Prisons regularly sponsor remedial reading and math programs for inmates needing such classes.

As anyone involved with adult education knows, however, there are still some students who cannot seem to learn to read. These may be such well-motivated persons that they return for remedial help year after year but still are not able to achieve their goal. They just seem unable to do this thing, to read. The likelihood is that these individuals belong to that segment of the population known as "learning disabled adults."

In some circles these adults are called "functional illiterates." They are among the most difficult of students to remediate, because of their long history of failure. They probably think they are "functionally" handicapped, that their illiteracy stems from some source within them that is permanently damaged. The LD adult has unique problems to cope with, but they are not necessarily irremediable.

Workshops are constantly offered, and books written, on the best methods to use with the LD adult. There have even been workshops dealing with the impact of right-hemisphere brain activities as these relate to possible aids in remediating the LD adult. One thing is certain. Just as children who exhibit learning disability need entirely unique and specific programs developed for their individual needs, so too do the LD adults. The same old programmed materials that they have already used with no apparent success are not sufficient for these handicapped individuals.

Some estimates are that as much as 80 percent of a population of adults reading at or below fourth-grade level are LD adults. Therefore, in a population of 30,000 who read at or below the fourth-grade level, about 24,000 would be considered LD adults.

It is estimated that out of a general population anywhere from 5 percent to 15 percent will be LD adults. Currently most newspapers are written at about a fourth-grade reading level to accommodate an increasingly illiterate population.

The influence of drugs on this LD adult program is significant. Many adults began experimenting with drugs as teen-agers. They may have become dependent on drugs or on alcohol at a very young age. Enough is known about these addictions to be certain that, in both instances, some brain cells are destroyed or there is significant alteration in performance levels. The original drug or alcohol problem may have occurred because the student was in an LBD program and felt caught there. Then the addiction compounded the problems.

The mother, herself an LBD teacher, speaks of her son. He is an LD student. He is on drugs. He is a senior in high school. He is afraid to go back to the regular program because he is sure he will fail. He is despondent at the thought of returning to LD for yet another year. She knows of several others like her son, all LD students. One is an alcoholic. He sees no future for himself. He cannot measure up to his parents' expectations of him for a career. He is not getting the kind of training in life skills, or job skills, that would provide him with the kind of satisfaction he seeks. His alcoholism will add to his LD problem, his inability to achieve those reading levels that would help him to extricate himself from this mess.

Some of these young adults become suicidal. Some succumb to the despair in different ways. Another way of dropping out of life is to become the "functionally illiterate" adult, the failure in the world of work.

There are CETA programs for a certain segment of adults who cannot get jobs and keep them because of their low academic performance. The clients in these programs must also be economically disadvantaged. Then they can be enrolled in remedial programs. They will also get job training and help in locating jobs. Even in these instances the career choices are limited and the expected range of pay is probably in the lower brackets. An added incentive in the CETA program, however, is the fact that the minimum wage is paid to the students for every hour spent in the program.

It is difficult for school systems to keep track of, to locate, the LBD students who leave their schools each year, either by dropping out or by graduating. It is a problem sometimes for school systems to locate, even with the help of their computers, all the LBD students currently enrolled in the system. Once the students have left, they are truly on their own. Nobody knows where they are.

The LBD teachers who work at the secondary school level or at the junior college or college level have an extraordinary opportunity to help young adults to face life with adequate skills. They have an opportunity to help these students learn to cope with problems and to make adjustments in frustrating situations. A part of any LBD programs at this level ought to include specific guidance techniques for these students. The students ought to be put in touch with agencies or organizations that can offer help and counseling after graduation.

There are, in most large communities, alternative schools for kids who have been expelled from the regular schools. Sometimes these schools are specifically for truants. These schools always require LBD teachers, as LBD students often exhibit the kinds of behaviors that lead to placement in them.

Secondary-level LBD teachers need to know a lot about the specific curriculums of the secondary schools. There is a move in some states that would require LBD teachers at the secondary level to be certified secondary teachers. For a time LBD teachers could teach any grade level; thus an LBD teacher might be certified for grades 1 to 12. Now, however, the elementary LBD teachers might be certified to teach in grades 1 to 8, and the secondary LBD teachers certified for grades 9 to 12. In any case, the LBD teacher needs to be familiar with the material being taught at a certain educational level and with some of the techniques for teaching the subject matter. It is helpful if the LBD teacher has actually taught in the regular programs at the level of the LBD classes he or she teaches. This is all part of the attempt to provide more fully developed programs for these students that will enable them to learn to function more successfully in their whole lives.

There are opportunities for LBD teachers in the CETA programs, in the prisons and in the vocational training schools. There is great emphasis at present in reducing the ranks of the "functionally illiterate" so that the unemployment problem in the country may be alleviated.

Vocational schools all over the country have implemented special programs of remediating learning problems. One of the major goals of the vocational schools is the improvement of academic levels of achievement. In many cases they hire LD staff for specialized strategies in remediation for a specific LD population.

The adult education planners are becoming increasingly aware that they need to employ LD personnel. Many such centers have made use of psychometric testing and have determined that the problems of some of their students defy remediation by means of the usual techniques. These students, they are coming to realize, need the help of LD specialists who understand about perceptional problems, know how to deal with visual-motor handicaps, and can handle communication problems. Some learning problems, it is now understood, are caused by just such areas of difficulty and need specially trained staff in order effectively to help the students.

Industry offers another possible source of employment for the LBD teacher. Some of the larger, multinational corporations employ guidance counselors and people to help employees improve their skills on the job. These have been largely successful. Most employees soon come to realize that advancement in the corporation depends upon improving skills and eagerly accept opportunities for educational improvement. When a worker receives a report back from a supervisor because it is not punctuated properly, or words are spelled incorrectly, or there are inaccurate statements, the worker will gladly accept some training in language skills in order to keep a job. The worker will also realize, within a short time, that other workers are being promoted and he or she is not being promoted. These large industries have affirmative action programs, so the worker must realize, also, that his or her inability to achieve advancement depends on the lack of certain skills and not on prejudices in the employer. The LD teacher looking for a rewarding job ought to find this a particularly satisfying one. The rewards for success are built into the achievement goals of the worker and into the promotion policies of the industry.

The factors of affirmative action and the requirement by the federal government that industry be equal opportunity employers have forced the issue of remediation at the industry level. More and more workers now come from minority groups and from situations of indigence. These are the people who have suffered the indignities of prejudice, welfare, and poverty all their lives. As has already been noted, these factors, whether singly or in combination, have had profound effects on the educational attitudes and performance of these victims. Their assimilation into the work force because of Federal mandates has caused problems for themselves and for their employers. It presents employers with a gigantic headache when they are required by law to hire and to promote people, in a system that professes to be judiciously fair and antidiscriminatory, when certain of these people cannot perform basic skills because they cannot read or write or do simple math operations. These corporations provide the skill-building training they see is needed. In some cases the programs are tax deductible for the companies. In other cases, the government may provide special funds for the remedial programs.

A business-management consultant says that the smaller companies also need remedial programs. They also must be equal opportunity employers and provide affirmative action programs. However, sometimes it is cheaper for companies with 500 or fewer employees simply to fire incompetent employees and hire new people. These employers need to be convinced of the greater efficiency and lower cost of providing remedial education on-site. They know they have a problem, but it remains for a skillful PR technique to "sell" them on the programs they need to initiate.

There are plenty of opportunities for LD or LBD teachers to find jobs. The whole field of adult education is loaded with opportunities for the enterprising LBD teacher. Again, there are grant funds available for almost any area that would improve the lives of the handicapped. The *Handicapped Funding Directory* lists these grant possibilities:[14]

1. *Rehabilitation training*—provided in fields directly related to vocational rehabilitation of the physically and mentally disabled.
2. *Rehabilitation services and facilities—special projects*—funds for client assistance, new careers for the handicapped, projects with industry, training services, etc.
3. *Rehabilitation services and facilities—basic support*—to provide vocational rehabilitation services to persons with mental and physical handicaps.

It is possible to find good sources of private funding in the *Grant Registers* of the local public libraries. These registers list alphabetically by states all the private foundations that offer grants. The indexes in the backs of the directories list the purposes of funding. All those foundations that give money for rehabilitation of the handicapped are listed alphabetically with page references.

There has been wide publicity given to the problem in the armed services of poor academic skills among the recruits. It seems there are many soldiers who cannot read, write, or do math problems. The army does hire people to operate remedial programs. Again this is a unique chance for the LD teacher. One needs to apply at the nearest Department of Labor office for the current Civil Service listing of jobs available in the desired specialty. The list is published periodically and provides information about the jobs in an entire region of the country that are available to certain professionals. Teaching posts are among these jobs. Very often they are on Army bases for the purpose of providing remedial programs. The Civil Service also provides job opportunities on some Indian reservations for teachers and for remedial education teachers.

There was the man who finally learned to read, and who said, "I can't get enough. I read everything I can get my hands on. They can say what they want. Just come and tangle with me."

For every evil under the sun
There is a remedy or there is none.
If there be one, seek till you find it;
If there be none, never you mind it.[15]

Chapter XI

Special Eds. Kids' Scenario

ADAM: *I am the smartest kid in my class.*

This is an exercise done in class with Ben, Adam, Lydia, Kim, Alice, and Chuck. It concerns the possible effects a new ice age would have on our civilization. The children discussed how we could survive and what effects such a crisis would have on our relations with the rest of the world.

CHUCK: We could live in underground houses and use oxygen tanks.

BEN: I'd take an airplane to another country.

ALICE: We could go to Africa.

BEN: We could use lasers to push the glacier off into outer space.

ADAM: We could change its course, so it would go to Russia.

KIM: We could hold the glacier back with a laser. Set up an invisible wall.

ALICE: Chop it up with lasers and put it on deserts. That would irrigate the deserts and there would be more farmland.

CHUCK: Everybody get a tent and move to the desert.

LYDIA: We could preserve some people in the ice, and then when we'd wake up the glacier would be gone.

BEN: Melt the glacier with lasers and turn the water into hydroelectric energy.

CHUCK: Sell pieces of it to Ayatollah Khomeini, so he could build an ice wall around Iran.

KIT: We could build a domed city for us to live in with enough radiation on the surface to keep the glacier back from us.

ALICE: We could set up a force field to keep the glacier back. We could use solar energy.

ADAM: We could grow what we needed inside the dome because we'd have solar power.

BEN: We'd have to become vegetarians. We couldn't stuff all those animals under the dome.

LYDIA: We could move to a space station, a satellite.

ALICE: We could go to the moon to live.

CHUCK: No, we'd freeze to death on the moon. And we couldn't breathe.

LYDIA: We could use astronaut food. They had T-bone steaks and grapes and all kinds of different things.

BEN: I have to have my meat.

ALICE: We could go on a diet till after the glacier leaves.

KIM: You could eat leftovers.

ADAM: You could have a food-bank, with freezers to store meat, and everybody in the world could get food from this bank.

CHUCK: We wouldn't need freezers with all that ice.

LYDIA: We could put carcasses on top of the ice, then drill holes and pull the carcasses down the holes when we need them.

BEN: I say every man for himself. Get your own food.

ALICE: They just have to survive like we are.

CHUCK: God put us on the richest land. If He had wanted those other people to have food He would have given them good farmland.

KIM: God said we should take care of our brothers.

LYDIA: I think it should be free for anybody. Anybody could go in, feel free to go in and get their food. For the whole world.

ADAM: We would have solar greenhouses and just go in and get our food when we need it.

That is a transcript of the creative solutions our LD friends explored for a world facing a crisis. They worked on some ideas for a threatened environment, of which they would be a part.

As special ed. kids they already know a lot about coping in a "threatening" environment. They know what they would like their real world and their fantasy world to be like.

IF ALL THE SEAS WERE ONE SEA

If all the seas were one sea,
What a *great* sea that would be!

And if all the trees were one tree,
What a *great* tree that would be!
And if all the axes were one axe,
What a *great* axe that would be!
And if all the men were one man,
What a *great* man that would be!
And if the *great* man took the *great* axe,
And cut down the *great* tree,
And let it fall into the *great* sea,
What a splish splash *that* would be![16]

Chapter XII

100 Frisbees From My Window

CHUCK: *The worst part of being in LD is when you get your report card and it's got LD on it.*

Is it possible to create schools where there would be no failures? No LBD kids? No special classes?

Milton Friedman was on the right track years and years ago when he and his wife first published their ideas for voucher schools. This concept is included in his recent book *Free to Choose.* There are all kinds of possibilities for more effective and more humane approaches to education if you let your mind do a little brainstorming.

Or, as the editor of *Creative Computing* magazine wrote, "If you would intuit, get intuit."[17]

One day Ben stood gazing out a window of my third-floor classroom. After a long time he turned to me and said, "I wonder what it would look like if I could throw a hundred Frisbees out this window."

Now just suppose that for the next school year the government gave you the $2,000 it spends on your annual education in public schools with the stipulation that you use the money to create the best of all possible schools. What would you do?

Perhaps, like Ben, you are a dreamer, an artist, an intuitive, creative person who feels frustrated and defeated in the kind of educational system we have set up for you. Yet, on the other hand, you may be discouraged because you really want to learn more and more about the world. You want to develop your mind to the limit of its ability for yourself, for your future, for the challenge you feel in the learning process. You are many people. You want many different things from your education. How could you do it satisfactorily with your $2,000?

Let your brainstorming ideas lead you out and away from the classroom windows that you know so well. Let them float, like a hundred different-colored Frisbees, away from the structure of the schools that you know to a hundred different destinations, a hundred different choices for an exciting education. A hundred different fantasies.

Let me share one of my favorite fantasies about schools with you. I am an LD teacher who would like to work myself out of a job. I think it would be fun to think up a way to beat the system, that is, to create a school where there would be no remediation, no special ed., no LBD.

I need to recall some of those "characteristics" of the LBD child in order to do this. What are they? How could I forget? The LBD child is, of course, *hyperactive, distractable, has a short attention span, may have perceptual problems, may have difficulty with eye and hand coordination,* etc., etc., etc. The LBD child may be very, very discouraged.

Maybe I will want a school without any sugar. *Absolutely no sugar.* There will be no pop, no bubble gum, no Cheetos, candy bars, lemon drops, Sugar Babies. Many people believe, you know, that diet has a lot to do with LD problems and that sugar is one of the worst enemies to the learning process that a child can come up against. Sugar may have a lot to do with hyperactivity, and that is one of the worst problems the LBD child faces.

So there will be no M & M's given for rewards in this school. There will be a lot of good nutritious health food, fruit and juice and nuts. And as far as rewards go, the school itself will be a rewarding experience for any child. Rewards for good behavior or for learning to do a certain task will not even be necessary because the school itself will be the reward.

There are limitless possibilities for schools that would meet every child's needs. Remember that each child is now in possession of the $2,000 for his or her own education. Would that be enough for all the children in the whole country, even those who are now currently enrolled in private schools and not receiving tax money for their education? If you consider that for every child in special ed. classes an average of about $3,000 is spent annually, and that hundreds more children are admitted to special ed. every year, the savings from the elimination of those classes would probably take care of the educational programs for those children in private schools at present.

There could be any kind of school you might want. My dream is that, on every block, in every neighborhood, there could be "cottage schools." Teachers could set up shop in their own homes. It would be one of the "cottage industries" Alvin Toffler talks about in *The Third Wave*. The teachers would work with one or two children at a time on a tutorial basis, providing the human elements of love and personal encouragement that are such very necessary factors in a child's education. The teachers might use home computers for remediation; there are some excellent remedial programs available in software for several of the major computers. These teachers would receive a predetermined portion of the child's "voucher" of $2,000. The teachers would be answerable to the parents and to the students for the types of programs offered and for the success rates of the students. Parents could simply take their money and their children elsewhere if quality educating was not being done by a teacher. The teachers would be accountable to their primary consumers for providing the best they could offer. The parents would have to be accountable to the teachers, on behalf of their children, for getting involved enough in the educational process to be intelligent consumers. The students themselves would feel more a part of the process, and the desire to get "their money's worth" would be one motivating factor. All concerned would definitely feel "ownership" of the educational process.

The return to many small neighborhood centers, for an hour or two of specialized person-to-person instruction daily, would eliminate busing. Both blacks and whites would feel more comfortable with their children getting some part of their education in the "home block" setting.

Very often the factor that has finally "broken" kids and forced them into LBD rooms later on in school is that they have never received enough personal attention to their educational needs. Sometimes they need a lot of time spent just on them. Sometimes they need a lot of attention given to their special ways of learning. Some kids learn things faster through auditory processes; others learn best through a visual process. There are those for whom a touch technique, the kinesthetic approach, is necessary for a time. There are those who have great difficulty with symbols, who have figure-ground difficulties and cannot even sort out separate letters from the background. There are those who cannot match symbols and sounds. There are those who "see" everything backwards. There are those who write everything backwards. Such children all have specific needs, but these needs do not constitute failure except in the context of schools as we now know them. The teachers in the schools we presently support do not have the time to help these children with their needs. They simply have too much to do and too many children to work with. It is inevitable that in the present setup many children become learning disabled.

In his book *Helping Children Overcome Learning Difficulties*, Jerome Rosner states what should be a positive goal for the parent of an LD child, given the kind of schools we now have. He says:

"My child will be able to read, write, spell, and do arithmetic as well as the other children in his class. His progress in school will be equal to the progress shown by the majority of his classmates."[18]

Elsewhere in his book he emphasizes that discouragement and failure are among the primary reasons why the child's will to learn eventually breaks down. The child can no longer keep up and so cannot cope with the schools we have.

If a child were removed from the setting in which he or she was constantly in competition with other children in a highly pressured system, the frustration of failing would be removed. If a child could have ample time with a teacher who knew how to help him or her, the idiosyncrasies he or she exhibited in the learning process would be taken in stride. If the child had only himself/herself to compete with, the onus of failure would be removed. The "cottage schools" could accomplish two things for the child who exhibited special learning needs. These schools would provide that a highly skilled teacher had plenty of time on a one-to-one level with the child, and the fear of failure to progress "as the majority of his classmates" would be removed.

Would the teachers in the "cottage schools" be highly trained specialists? They would have to be if they wanted to compete for the voucher money. They would have to seek and find the courses that would enable them to become really fine teachers, not get just any education degree from any college or university that happened to be close by. They would have to advertise their specialties. They would have to compete in the marketplace for consumers to buy their "product" like any other vendor of wares, the "wares" here being educational programs. They could build up their following of "satisfied customers" like other successful capitalists.

Some of these teachers would probably be interested in specific problem areas of the learning disabled child. There would then be specialists who were involved, not in remediation, but in providing adequate methods in the instructional process for this type of child to learn on an individual basis. There would be no learning disabled child, because the "disability" exists only in relation to "other" children in schools as we now have them.

Thus, a child would spend, say, two hours alone with the teacher, or with one or two other children, at the "cottage school" every day. *Then* the child would attend the major computer center downtown.

Here is where my Frisbees get almost out of sight. I cannot keep up with them. The ideas, the possibilities for children with learning problems are so fantastic that the brainstorming gets out of hand.

I am thinking of specifically three computers that have educational programs, that could be programmed by the students themselves, that have graphic designs. These are the TRS-80, the PET, and APPLE 11. They all use BASIC language and are capable of programming by students and teachers.

Computers are mind-expanding facilitators. They allow the programmer to learn *how to think.* They involve the user in the process of learning. They do not simply teach facts, although they can be used for this function. They are more than calculators. The user becomes involved in thought processes.

Karen Billings says in the magazine *Microcomputing:*

Teaching with a microcomputer has given me a chance to experience a potentially important resource in American education. I see the students excited by its interactivity, open-endedness and versatility in presenting text, sound and graphics. They are really being exposed to a "mind-multiplier."

The students are much less afraid of the computers than are their teachers. They have more access and more time to get involved. Programming gives the student a chance to control the computer rather than being controlled. It emphasizes the process as well as the product. I can recall few other instances in school where a student describes an action, then executes it on command. Programming has enabled some of my students to share "intellectual products" with each other.[19]

In dealing with children who have learning problems, we are dealing with a blocking at a certain level of learning, at a certain developmental stage in the learning process. These children need more help, perhaps, at one particular stage of development. They become failures when they see the majority surpass them *at this level,* and then the blockage may become permanent. They are never free, then, to become involved in the *excitement* of learning. They never learn to learn. As Piaget says:

The ideal of education is not to teach the maximum, to maximize the results, but above all to learn to learn, to learn to develop, and to learn to continue to develop after leaving school.[20]

Computers are being used in some school systems, primarily with gifted kids. However, school systems are limited in the funds they can provide for really extensive use of the microcomputers by all students. If a good portion of voucher money was paid into a good computer center that would be accessible to all students of a metropolitan area for an hour or two a day, there could be enough variety in programming to meet the needs of all students on an individual basis.

One needs to recall here the theory that there are many more gifted kids than we realize who wind up in LD classes, or in BD rooms. As Nan Johnson of Good Apple, Inc. puts it, "We may just not speak the same language as some of these LD kids,"[21] and they are the losers in the present system. They may very well be gifted kids who are blocked at a certain developmental level, but who have now been programmed into failure.

In her workshops on "gifted children" for Good Apple, Nan tells the story of the autistic child who was totally without language activities from birth. This child painted so beautifully that some of her paintings were hung in museums. At about the age of six her parents took her to a special clinic, where she began to learn language skills. As she learned to talk her artistic ability decreased proportionately. By the time she gained full control of language patterns she was drawing stick figures.

Nan tells also the story of the children on the Navajo Indian Reservation. An old Indian man told her sadly how the young had forgotten the beautiful patterns for blankets that for hundreds of years the Navajo women had woven and passed from one generation to the next. Little Navajo girls had stood behind their grandmothers' shoulders as soon as they could stand and learned the patterns. When they were about ten or eleven they themselves began weaving the patterns into blankets. Since the children have been going to Anglo schools they have lost the ability to remember the patterns. The old Indian told Nan that if this contribution of the Navajos to the world is to be continued, the patterns must be put down in books.

Children with street survival skills have a language and patterning process all their own. They have developed intuitive skills to a very high degree of proficiency. They are gifted children in their area of need and expertise. They often are failures in the school system.

What if our LBD children are really gifted children, and we simply do not speak the same language as they do?

Maybe these kids could speak BASIC. There are programs and possibilities for program development on microcomputers that can help expand the intuitive, creative potential of the users. In his Pulitzer Prize-winning book *The Dragons of Eden*, Carl Sagan reviews the evolutionary development of the brain. He remarks on the growing awareness of the right hemisphere of the brain as the center of intuitive skills, of spatial awareness, of deductive reasoning. In his book *The Brain, the Last Frontier*, Dr. Richard Restak continues the examination into the theory that the right hemisphere controls creative thought. Dr. Sagan deplores the dismal approach to education we now subscribe to. He feels that our schools are places where an inflexible, rigid instructional mode is responsible for the students' lack of enthusiasm for learning. He also talks about the many exciting and educational functions of computers and about all that students could learn from them, from physics to computer graphics.

In another article in *Microcomputing*, George Ropes and Henry Gaylord say this:

"A school contemplating a microcomputer program should set its sights on accomplishing at least one of the following goals:

Teaching students to write programs
Providing opportunities to learn through simulations and games
Teaching subject matter, such as mathematics, science, social studies
Building skills in vocabulary, spelling, computation, shape recognition
Drill and practice on basics."[22]

There are programs on these microcomputers for learners with "perceptual" problems. There are specific programs for the recognition of shapes and letters. There are soundware programs that could aid in sound and symbol match exercises as well as enable the user to produce some creative effects with sound. The programmer can play melodies on the computers, change the pitch of notes, and control the beats of the notes. There are programs in color graphics. The PET sells a "light pen" that plugs into the computer and can be used by any child in applications directly on the screen. The graphics programs engage the programmer in the actual building of three-dimensional shapes.

In the magazine *Recreational Computing,* Don Inman designed the following program for his daughter who was in kindergarten. Programs of this type could be used very well by the child who needed practice in developing perceptual skills.[23]

I would expect that a regular feature of this educational system, with the happy marriage between the "cottage schools" and the computer center, would be that the teacher from the "cottage school" would be totally familiar with the child's program at the computer center. Indeed, this teacher should be involved in the testing and planning for the specific programs the child uses at the center. What kind of tests?

There is one especially significant profile of intelligence that might help the teacher-parent-student team to plan an exceptionally good program for the child with learning problems. It is not a test of quantitative information or content. It is not a conventional IQ test. It is called the "Structure of Intellect Learning Abilities Test."[24] It was developed by Mary Meeker, who based the test on J. Guilford's theory of intellect.

Seven shapes are drawn on the left edge of the video screen.

One of these seven shapes is then randomly chosen and it appears in the lower right corner of the screen along with the question, "WHAT IS THE NUMBER OF THE MATCHING FIGURE?"

The user then keys in the number of the shape which he/she thinks the random shape matches. The ENTER key is then pressed. The random shape then moves vertically and horizontally to a position adjacent to the chosen shape.

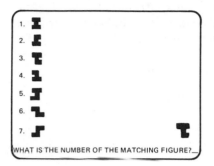

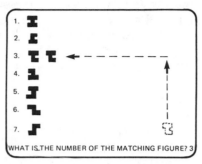

A message then tells whether the choice was correct or not.

My daughter is able to match the shape 100% of the time. After such success, the level of difficulty should be increased. This can be done by adding a method of timing the responses or by making the shapes more complex.

Guilford contributed the theories on divergent thinking skills and convergent thinking skills to the body of knowledge about the functions of the brain. The divergent thinking skills are associated with the intuitive, creative activities of the right hemisphere. The convergent thinking skills are linked to left-hemisphere activities such as linear thinking, cognitive memory, and logical thought. The higher-level activities are those associated with the right hemisphere, such as evaluative processes and the ability to synthesize and analyze.

The test features five parts. The test on cognition has nine subtests. The memory test has four subtests, as do both the evaluative test and the test in convergent products. The test in divergent products has three subtests. The results of these various tests can be grouped for a diagnostic profile in reading and math.

A total learning program could be mapped out for any child with such a comprehensive testing device. It touches on virtually all functions of the brain and gives information that would enable the planner to know exactly what areas of functioning needed most help. With the microcomputers available to do just about any kind of work for the programmer, the teacher could plan the precise program to develop strengths and overcome weaknesses in any learning area for a given student. Both right- and left-hemisphere activities could be plotted into the child's computer program and reinforced by the teacher in the "cottage school."

The possibilities are endless. To put it in BASIC:

```
NEW
OK
1 PRINT "I"
2 PRINT "CAN"
3 PRINT "LEARN"
4 PRINT "TO"
5 PRINT "LEARN"
RUN
I
CAN
LEARN
TO
LEARN
OK
RUN
```

There could, conceivably, be some voucher money left. Maybe parents could pool this money to provide some really fun things for the kids to do. These fun things might even be educational.

There could be a circus operated by the children. Professional clowns and other performers would help the kids prepare for the circus events, but the kids would put on the show themselves. There would be things the handicapped kids could feel comfortable doing. The circus would be in a centralized area and, sometime during the year, all kids would get a chance to perform. Some part of each day, after the more formal educational functions were dispensed with, could be spent in practicing acts, making costumes, working at the concession stands, cleaning up, decorating the tents, or joining in the parades.

Probably one of the most popular places would be the local sports center, where kids could go to swim, play ball, do gymnastics, or skate.

There would be physical education teachers specially trained in motor coordination skills to work with all the participants, but especially the handicapped.

There could be a performing arts center. Many children could have the opportunity to take music, dance, or drama lessons from the actual artists who perform in the local theater groups.

A marvelous centralized library would offer much more than books to children. Here there would be story-telling activities, puppet shows, old movies, educational films, and much, much more.

An art museum would display children's paintings next to those of Rembrandt and Picasso. Space in the museum could be given over to local artists, who would receive part of the voucher fee to teach the children art.

There could be a science center where kids could work on projects, maybe for a really big science fair. The materials they needed would be there. Local scientists would share the skills of their discipline with them and supervise them.

A meeting hall could be used for regular lectures for the students of political history, geopolitics, civics. Kids could stage their own debates here, set up town meetings, get involved in the political process.

There might be opportunities for the students to share the facilities of a local newspaper to put out one of their own. They might have air time on one of the commercial radio stations or on NPR. They could produce their own show, write their own commercials, with the expert help of local broadcasters.

There could be an animal center staffed by veterinarians who would help the children understand the importance of good animal care.

There might be career centers set up by local industries, with role-playing components built into the projects. Junior Achievement would be a part of this unit.

The science museums would continue to be places of fascination and inspiration for children. Many kinds of museums could be developed that would encourage student planning and involvement.

Once you start brainstorming possibilities, you can get quite carried away with the excitement of it all. The many-colored Frisbees can lead you far, far away from the top floor of the old brick school.

But, you must be saying, on $2,000 could so much be done?

Imagine a system of 20,000 schoolchildren. If each one of them chipped in $500 to the computer center, there would be a $10,000,000 computer center, and that ought to be adequate. The PETs, APPLE IIs and TRS-80s cost around $1,000 each, give or take a few hundred dollars difference between the models. And once the initial purchase has been made these will last, with care, for a very long time; that initial expense would not need to be duplicated for a while. The software, at anywhere from $5 to $40 for existing programs, would be a continuing expense.

So, assuming that $500 has been used up from the voucher money, that leaves $1,500 more for educational programs. Whatever the parent-teacher-child teams chose as most beneficial for the kids would get the bulk of the rest of the money. If they chose a "cottage teacher" who charged $500 per pupil for one or two hours of individualized tutoring daily, that would leave another thousand for the optional programs. The parents would buy into the programs they and their children liked the best. If, on the other hand, they opted for a specialist who charged $1,000 per pupil for an hour or two of daily "cottage class," that would leave them only $500 for the rest of the program. A lot could be offered to their children with just the $500. Given, again, the 20,000 students in a system, the pooling of voucher money at even $100 per child would yield $2,000,000.

This educational program could *earn* money. There is money to be made from the development, copyrighting, and sale of software programs. The teachers and students alike could develop this market. Teachers already have money-making opportunities from the sale of ideas to certain educational magazines and, particularly, to publications like *Good Apple*. There is every reason to believe that this market could be expanded if the teachers found it profitable enough.

One of the major strengths of the optional programs is that they would use professionals from each field *in their own settings* to accomplish an educational task. These people would be paid for their part in the instructional program. They would have the materials at hand to do the job they wanted to do. They would facilitate learning, provide the ideas to arouse curiosity, and encourage the timid to participate. These would not be pass/fail programs. They would be participatory-learning centers staffed by experts and artists.

Thus, after the information from the intelligence profile had been gathered, the parent-teacher-child team might decide that Adam would go to a "cottage school" for two hours in the early morning. Then he might ride the local bus downtown for his mid-morning session at the computer center. After his two hours there, Adam would take a shuttle bus to the performing arts center for a ballet lesson. The shuttle buses might be funded by voucher money by a group of parents. When his ballet lesson was over, he could walk or ride the shuttle bus to the gym for an hour of swimming. Adam's last session of the day might be spent reading in the library, after which he would take either the shuttle or a city bus home.

Kit, however, might go to the circus first thing in the morning. The rest of her day might be programmed so that she went to art class at the museum of art, then to the science center where she worked on biology experiments, then to the radio station where she worked on making commercials with a group of other students. She might then go to the computer center for her work there and keep her appointment with her tutor last thing in the afternoon.

There would be more than enough exciting, inspirational, educational things for the kids to do in a day's time. There wouldn't be enough time in the day to learn all that one wanted to learn. There would be no scheduling problem of trying to keep kids busy for a six- or seven-hour day whether they learned anything or not. There would be so many opportunities for children to learn exciting things from masters in their fields that it would take any one child several years to sample all that could be offered. And there would be the advantage also that a specially gifted child in any one field could stay with a certain master, a musician, for instance, for as long as the parent-teacher-master-child team thought it advisable.

Part of the pooled voucher money could go toward the purchase of nutritious snacks at each center. Even the circus would have to provide healthful food at the concession stands. *No cotton candy,* enormous blobs of sticky-sweet spun sugar, would be sold at *this* circus.

The best feature of this program would be that it was totally individualized. And at the computer center, as well as in the tutorial setting, the child would not be competing with anyone other than the self. This might even be so at most of the optional centers. The child would progress at the speed comfortable to himself/herself. No one else need ever know. No child would be measured, ever again, in comparison with "the progress shown by the majority of his classmates."

The "whole child" would be touched by a creative instructional program. It would be possible to provide a system of education that would be based on Gestalt theory. According to this theory, the elements of a "whole" can be understood only in relation to a prior concept of the "whole." The human being is made up of mind and feeling. The awareness of both these functions is essential to the development of an effective educational program. This is "confluent" education. As George Isaac Brown says in *The Live Classroom,* "Thinking about education in confluent ways can help restore revitalizing juices to education. Man has a mind. Man has feeling. To separate the two is to deny all that man is. To integrate the two is to help man realize what he might be."[25]

The children who would benefit most from a system based on confluent educational theory would be those who are most crippled by the present educational models. The gifted children and the special ed. kids stand to benefit the most from confluent education. The children who exhibit some form of learning problems could "expand" the most.

According to Jerome Rosner in *Helping Children Overcome Learning Difficulties,* the problem learners, especially the hyperactive kids, have been treated by a lot of different methods by a lot of different teachers in a lot of different classrooms. It seems almost as if any teacher who is convinced that a particular method will work with these kids has had success in helping the disabled learners. There are teachers who are passionately devoted to certain techniques and realize success in their implementation.

Dr. Art Ulene on the NBC *Today* show in August, 1980, reported on a school for hyperactive children where the teacher had really great success in helping the students by means of a method of programmed rest periods. The children "rested" for a certain period each day, and during that time the teacher talked very quietly to them, encouraging them to a deeper state of rest. Several of the students had made remarkable changes in behavior and learning patterns.

On CBS *60 Minutes* in October, 1979, attention was focused on a teacher in Chicago who had left the public schools and started her own school for inner-city kids. She was passionately concerned with teaching the "King's English" to her students. They were reading Shakespeare and Chaucer and loving it. She had succeeded.

William Buckley, Jr. reported in a syndicated column in December, 1979, on a program begun by two teachers in a public school in Camden, South Carolina, in 1964. It was based on a form of teacher-pupil contracting and relied on the utmost confidentiality. It worked. Students were improving.

The point is that any teacher who was passionately convinced of a certain approach to learning could do a good job of helping kids to learn, given the right incentives for the teacher. The "cottage schools" could do a tremendous amount of good for children with learning problems because the teachers would have a lot of "ownership" in the success of each school.

Joseph Pearce says in *The Crack in the Cosmic Egg,*

The asking of a question with passionate concern for its answer, a concern which demands life investment, suggests a door which will sooner or later be found. Whether it is successfully opened to the public is another matter, but if a current world view can *accommodate* a new synthesis, the new idea may prove to be the case. A new idea fails if it involves too great a sacrifice of invested belief. If the new idea triggers a passionate enough pursuit to make suspension or abandonment of previous beliefs, or current criteria worth the risk, however, the new idea can *change* the reality structure.[26]

The reality structure is a school system that has a built-in coefficient for failure. The gifted children and the special ed. kids are the big losers. But no child is well served in a structure that does not accommodate change.

Jerome Bruner says in *Toward a Theory of Instruction:*

"I shall take it as self-evident that each generation must define afresh the nature, direction, and aims of education to assure such freedom and rationality as can be attained for a future generation. For there are changes both in circumstances and in knowledge that impose constraints on and give opportunities to the teacher in each succeeding generation. It is in this sense that education is in constant process of invention. I should like particularly to comment upon four changes in our own time that require consideration in thinking about education.

The first of these derives from our increasing understanding of man as a species. . . .

A second basis for redefining education is the increase in our understanding of the nature of individual mental growth. . . .

Third, there is reason to believe that we have come to understand the process of education somewhat more clearly than before. . . .

Finally, and most obviously, the rate of change in the society in which we live forces us to redefine how we shall educate a new generation. . . ."[27]

In *Broca's Brain,* Carl Sagan tells us, "We are at a crossroads in human history. Never before has there been a moment so simultaneously perilous and promising. We are the first species to have taken our evolution into our own hands. For the first time we possess the means for intentional or inadvertent self-destruction. We also have, I believe, the means for passing through this stage of technological adolescence into a long-lived, rich and fulfilling maturity for all the members of our species. But there is not much time to determine to which fork of the road we are committing our children and our future."[28]

The brainstorming has exhausted me mentally. The children have left the classroom for the day, and I can still see some of Ben's many-colored Frisbees dancing in the distance. From the third-floor windows I can see the shapes they form as they twist and spin and gyrate. They become part of a lovely three-dimensional design, something like these:[29]

PLOTTER GRAPHICS

By Nick Mykris with David Ballew, Dept.
of Mathematics, South Dakota School of
Mines and Technology.

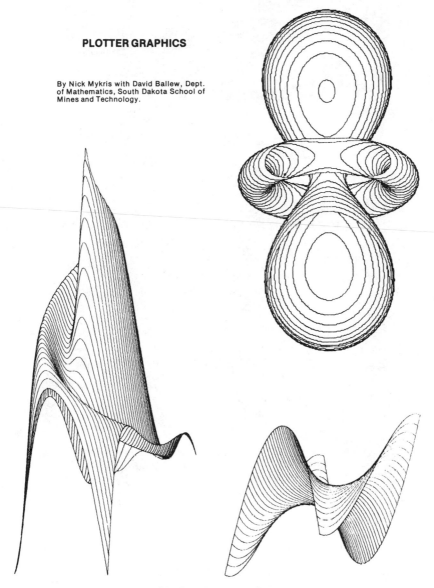

11. Creative computing

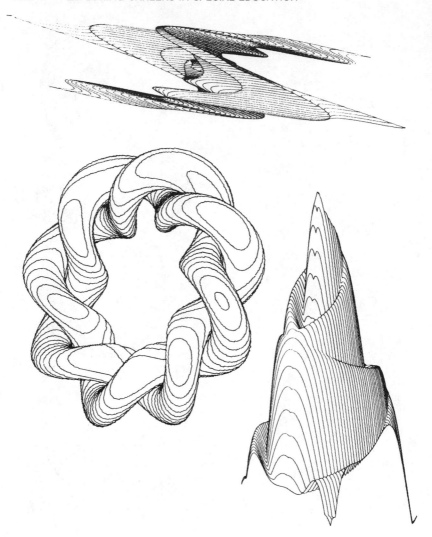

Endnotes

1. *Key Federal Regulations Affecting the Handicapped—1975–76* (U.S. Department of Health, Education, and Welfare, Sept. 1977).
2. Gerald Wallace and James M. Kauffman, *Teaching Children With Learning Problems* (Columbus, Ohio: Charles E. Merrill Publishing Company, 1973), p.10ff.
3. Ibid.
4. *The Real Mother Goose* (The British Commonwealth: Rand McNally and Company, 1961), p.85.
5. Richard DeMille, *Put Your Mother on the Ceiling* (New York: Penguin Books, 1977), p.130.
6. *The Real Mother Goose*, p.45.
7. Wallace and Kauffman, op. cit.
8. *The Real Mother Goose*, p.12.
9. *Exceptional Children* (Denver: Love Publishing Company), February, 1980.
10. *ERIC: The ERIC Clearinghouse on Handicapped and Gifted Children* (The Council for Exceptional Children: Reston, Virginia)
11. Ibid.
12. Burton J. Eckstein, *Handicapped Funding Directory* (Research Grant Guides: P.O. Box 357, Oceanside, NY) p.89.
13. *The Real Mother Goose*, p.30.
14. *Eckstein*, op. cit. p.94ff.
15. *The Real Mother Goose*, p.32.
16. *The Real Mother Goose*, p.53.
17. Eugene Raudsepp, "New Look at the Creative Process," *Creative Computing*, August, 1980. Vol 6, No. 8, p.46.
18. Jerome Rosner, *Helping Children Overcome Learning Difficulties* (U.S.A.: Walker Publishing Co.) 1953, p.23.
19. Karen Billings, "Microcomputers in Education," *Microcomputing*, June, 1980. p.100ff.

20. Jean Piaget, *The Child and Reality* (New York: Penguin Books, 1972), p.30.
21. Nan Johnson, Good Apple, Inc., (Carthage, Illinois).
22. George Ropes & Henry Gaylord, "Bringing Microcomputers Into Schools," *Microcomputing*, June, 1980. p.104.
23. Don Inman, "Match Me," *Recreational Computing*, Nov.–Dec., 1979, Vol. 8, No. 3, p.11ff.
24. SOI Institute, 214 Main Street, El Segundo, California 90245, 1975.
25. George Isaac Brown, *The Live Classroom* (New York: The Viking Press, 1975) p.108.
26. Joseph Pearce, *The Crack in the Cosmic Egg* (New York: Pocket Books, 1971) p.67.
27. Jerome Bruner, *Toward a Theory of Instruction* (Cambridge, Mass.: Belknap Press, 1966), p.67.
28. Carl Sagan, *Broca's Brain* (New York: Random House, 1979) p.39ff.
29. Nick Mykris & David Ballew, "Plottergraphics," *Creative Computing*, August, 1980, Vol 6, No 8, p.72ff.

Bibliography

Billings, Karen. "Microcomputers in Education," *Microcomputing,* June, 1980.

Brown, George Isaac. *The Live Classroom.* New York: Viking Press, 1975.

Bruner, Jerome. *Toward a Theory of Instruction.* Cambridge, MA: Belknap Press, 1966.

DeMille, Richard. *Put Your Mother on the Ceiling.* New York: Penguin Books, 1977.

Eckstein, Burton J. *Handicapped Funding Directory.* Oceanside, NY: Research Grant Guides, 1980.

ERIC: The ERIC Clearinghouse on Handicapped and Gifted Children. Reston, VA: The Council for Exceptional Children, 1980.

Exceptional Children. Denver: Love Publishing Company, February, 1980.

Friedman, Milton and Rose. *Free to Choose.* New York: Harcourt Brace Jovanovich, 1979, 1980.

Good Apple. Carthage, IL, 1979.

Inman, Don. "Match Me." *Recreational Computing,* Nov.–Dec. 1979, Vol. 8, No. 3.

Johnson, Nan. *Good Apple,* Inc., Carthage, IL.

Key Federal Regulations Affecting the Handicapped 1975–76. U.S. Department of Health, Education, & Welfare, September, 1977.

Learning Magazine. Boulder, CO: Education Today Company, Inc., 1979.

Mykris, Nick, and Ballew, David. "Plottergraphics." *Creative Computing,* August, 1980, Vol. 6, No.8.

Pearce, Joseph. *The Crack in the Cosmic Egg.* New York: Pocket Books, 1971.

Piaget, Jean. *The Child and Reality.* New York: Penguin Books, 1972.

Raudsepp, Eugene. "New Look at the Creative Process." *Creative Computing,* August, 1980, Vol. 6, No. 8.

Real Mother Goose, The. Rand McNally & Company, 1961.

Restak, Richard M., M.D. *The Brain: The Last Frontier.* Garden City, NY: Doubleday, 1979.

Rosner, Jerome. *Helping Children Overcome Learning Difficulties.* Walker Publishing Co., 1975.

Ropes, George, and Gaylord, Henry. "Bringing Microcomputers Into Schools." *Microcomputing,* June, 1980.

Sagan, Carl. *The Dragons of Eden.* New York: Random House, 1977.

————. *Broca's Brain.* New York: Random House, 1979.

Smith, Linda G. *Doodling Your Way to Better Recall.* Novato, CA: Academy Therapy Publications, 1979.

Toffler, Alvin. *The Third Wave.* New York: William Morrow & Company, 1980.

Wallace, Gerald, and Kauffman, James M. *Teaching Children with Learning Problems.* Columbus, OH: Charles E. Merrill Publishing Company, 1973.

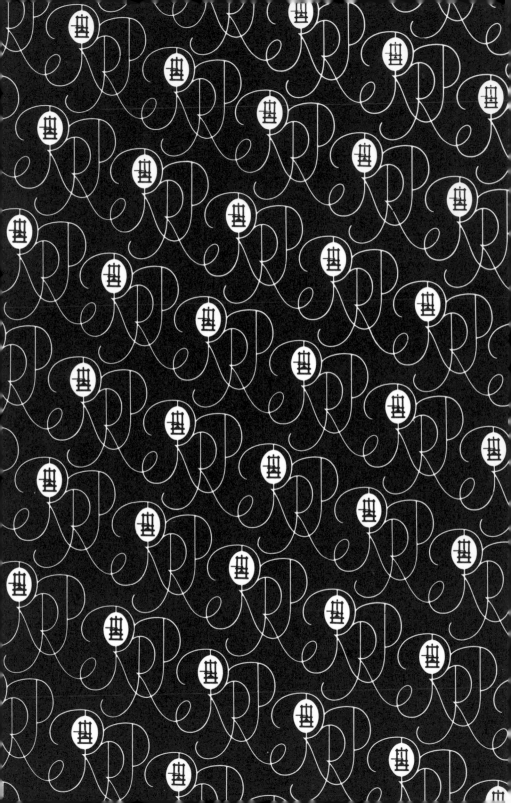